PRAYER
WILL CHANGE YOUR WORLD

David Hoffman

The effective prayer of a righteous man can accomplish much.
(James 5:16)

He will call to me and I will answer him, I will be with him in trouble, I will rescue and honor him.
(Psalm 91:15)

PRAYER
WILL CHANGE YOUR WORLD

David Hoffman

Pastor Dave Hoffman may be contacted at:
Foothills Christian Church
350-B Cypress Ave.
El Cajon, CA 92020
(619) 442-7728

Publisher information:
CSN Books
P.O. Box 1450
Pine Valley, CA 91962
Toll Free: 1-800-636-7276
www.csnbooks.com

Printed in the United States of America.

Sixth Edition 2018

DEDICATION

To those who have gone before and challenged me to pray: A. W. Tozer, E. M. Bounds, Reese Howells, George Mueller, Leonard Raven-hill, Hudson Taylor, Charles Finney, Andrew Murray, Smith Wigglesworth, John Hyde, and my mother Ruth Hoffman.

Every one of these saints knew the importance of prayer, and the result was that our Lord used them mightily. Their lives affected many for the cause of Christ.

TABLE OF CONTENTS

CHAPTER ONE

Prayer: The Beginning

No doubt you are reading this book on prayer because you possess a God-given desire to pray. You know that without prayer your Christian experience will never develop beyond Christian infancy.

If you have read the accounts of Christians who have been mightily used by our Lord, you know that prayer was always a large part of their lives. In the Gospel of Luke, it is clear that prayer played a major part in the daily life of Jesus. His disciples, observing Jesus day after day, understood it was through prayer that He received His wisdom, strength and direction from the Father.

Naturally, the disciples asked Jesus to teach them how to pray.

> *It happened that while Jesus was praying in a certain place, after He had finished, one of his disciples said to him, Lord, teach us to pray just as John also taught his disciples.*

(Luke 11:1)

In over thirty years as a Christian, and over 25 years as a pastor, I have come to know that prayer is the single most important activity of our Christian life!

Why?

Prayer brings power, strength, joy, peace, wisdom, and the kingdom of heaven into our daily activities. You and I can do nothing without God (John 15:5). Therefore, we can do very little without prayer. Although most Christians understand the value of prayer, they often find it difficult to fit prayer into their busy lives, and I was no exception.

Some years ago I believe the Lord spoke to me during my morning devotions through one little verse.

> *For the Kingdom of God does not consist in words but in power.*
>
> (1 Corinthians 4:20)

After years in the ministry it had become obvious to me that I didn't have a natural gift for teaching or preaching, and I did not have a great vision for ministry ideas.

My brother Mark and I had started our church 6 years earlier, and nothing much was happening. Believe me when I tell you that if hard work alone could have brought about success, the church would have been growing. I can tell you that I was literally exhausted. But after all those years of hard work, our church was still very small and doing little for the Kingdom of our Lord. I was very discouraged.

This passage in Corinthians changed my thinking. I didn't have to be brilliant, tall, good-looking, charismatic, a gifted orator, or funny to do great things for God. What I needed was the power of God, His influence working in my life and the ministries of the church.

As a matter of fact, I knew several pastors whose messages were powerfully affecting people, but they would have never been given a good grade by any of my preaching professors. I knew individuals who had little training or, it seemed, natural giftings, but God was mightily using them. I'll never forget Jim, a meat packer in Dubuque, Iowa. If you had met him you would have never have guessed that every Wednesday night hundreds came to hear him teach God's Word. He'd never gone to

Bible School or seminary but people came by the hundreds to hear him teach God's Word. Why were these things happening? Simply because God was there, as was His presence and His power.

Think how many Christian messages, tapes, books, radio programs, crusades, church "how to" materials, and TV programs have been produced in America within the last fifty years. I would guess that more words have been spoken and written about Jesus to the last two generations in America than any other two generations in the last two thousand years. And with all this effort what has been the outcome? In America, we only convert about 2% of the population each year, the same percent that die (Barna Research).

Why are we failing to win America for Christ? The answer, "The Kingdom of God does not consist in words but in power" (1 Corinthians 4:20). And what is the Kingdom of God? Is it not simply the presence and the power of the King?

The American church is full of words, but words do not necessarily bring the presence and power of God. But where God's presence is, where His power is, God's Kingdom advances, people come to Christ, and they are healed and delivered.

Friend, each of us possesses the key in releasing God's presence and power into our family, church and community. That's why I consider prayer the single most important activity of the Christian life.

Prayerlessness for us as Christians is unacceptable. Why? Simply again, because it brings God's presence, which brings His influence, strength, wisdom, discernment, and healing into our lives and the world around us.

Consider what we are told in James 4:2,

You do not have because you do not ask.

These eight words contain the secret to the spiritual poverty and powerlessness of the average American Christian church.

Too often Christians ask, "Why do I have so little victory over sin in my life?" "Where is God's direction and anointing?" "Why do I get defeated so easily?" "Why aren't more people getting saved and baptized in our churches?" "Why isn't there more conviction of sin?" "Where are the volunteers to minister in our churches?" "Why aren't we seeing more healings and miracles in our churches?"

God answers these questions with these nine words:

"You do not have because you do not ask."

It is my conviction that Satan's strategy with God's people has always been to whisper, "Don't ask, don't seek, trust yourself, your instincts and gut feelings."

The truth is, the devil is not frightened or intimidated by human wisdom, zeal, or education. But he knows when God's people pray in total dependence on the Lord, he's in trouble!

PRAYER PRODUCES RESULTS

Martin Luther prayed four hours each day because he believed he could never accomplish all that was expected of him without prayer.

When I was in seminary, I discovered that when I consistently spent time each morning in prayer and devotion, my grades went up dramatically. By the time I graduated, I was spending considerable time praying every day and, as a result, receiving straight A's in my coursework.

Because of prayer, my seminary experience was a success. But, as I began my life in the ministry as a youth pastor thirty years ago, my prayer life waned.

Why did this happen?

Well, it is easy to list the "reasons": A different environment, no more school pressures, my daily routine changed, more social demands, etc. These are all great excuses, but that is all they remain—excuses.

I have always known it was important to pray, but the challenge still remained to be consistent in my daily prayer.

I cannot possibly tell you how many times I have failed to diligently pray. How often were my efforts in serving God hampered by my unwillingness to put in time on my knees? I can relate to Paul's words,

> *For the willing is present in me, but the doing of the good is not.*
>
> (Romans 7:18)

As Jesus said,

> *The spirit is willing, but the flesh is weak.*
>
> (Mark 14:38)

My friend, I have found prayer to be a struggle even though I know God has called me to a life of prayer! It has not been easy to discipline myself to regular, significant prayer times. There always seems to be someone or something to interrupt my prayer schedule.

The reality is that sometimes prayer can feel like work, and frequently we just do not feel like doing it.

PRAYER PRODUCES KNOWLEDGE OF CHRIST

Most of us have not been called to a prayer ministry, but to prayer. We have been called to get alone with God on a regular basis so God's love, mercy, wisdom, strength, and direction will be manifested in our lives.

That is the challenge of prayer.

In Colossians 4:2, Paul tells us,

> *Devote yourselves to prayer, keeping alert in it with an attitude of thanksgiving.*

The word "devote" means to apply attention, time, or oneself to some activity. The activity we need to apply attention to is prayer, one of the most important parts of our Christian experience.

In Philippians 2, Paul says Christians ought to be "united" and "intent on one purpose." I believe this one purpose is knowing God. His heart and His will for all aspects of our lives, including every circumstance and relationship. Having God's heart and knowing God's will naturally changes our view of the world and affects every area of relationship with others.

Paul tells us in Philippians 3:8,

> *I count all things to be loss in view of the surpassing value of knowing Christ Jesus my Lord, for whom I have suffered the loss of all things, and count them but rubbish so that I may gain Christ.*

What does Paul want us to gain?

Jesus Christ.

Paul is already saved, so what Paul wants is to know Christ—to have His desires, His love, wisdom, strength, mercy and discernment.

Practically, how do we get to know Christ?

By spending time with Him.

Read His Word and talk with Him in prayer.

Faith is not just knowledge. It is a relationship with Jesus. You may know things about Billy Graham, but you will never really know him unless you spend many quality hours with him as a friend.

I frequently hear men and women in troubled marriages say, "I just don't know my spouse anymore," or "There just isn't any love between us anymore," or "We do not have anything in common." The real problem in these marriages is that somewhere along the line these couples stopped talking with one another and stopped spending quality time together.

They grew apart and fell out of touch.

You and I have been called to be imitators of Christ (1 Corinthians 11:1), but we can never imitate Christ if we do not know Him. If we truly know Christ—His heart and His will—then we will be able to bring Jesus into every situation, crisis, and relationship.

We can never *"know Him and the power of His resurrection"* (Philippians 3:10) without spending time with God in prayer. As we devote ourselves to prayer, God transforms us, changing our desires and thoughts to parallel His (2 Corinthians 3:18). That is why prayer is the single most important activity of our Christian lives.

BE PERSISTENT IN YOUR PURSUIT OF CHRIST

As you read this book, I pray God stirs and awakens your heart to the importance of prayer.

For most of us, prayer is a challenge. I have spent the last 35+ years trying to become a man who prays and accomplishes much for our Lord Jesus (James 5:16).

It has been a struggle, but, I pray more today than I did just a few years ago.

It is my belief that as you begin to understand and practice the Biblical foundations shared in this book your prayer life will increase from what it is today.

Prayer is challenging, but with a good theology of prayer and some simple, practical guidelines, prayer can become what our Lord intended it to be—an exciting time of refreshing, anointing, and ministry to us, our families, and the world around us.

CHAPTER TWO

Do You Believe in Prayer?

Dear Reader, do you believe in prayer?

This is a very pertinent question for all Christians in the United States, especially given the moral decay we witness in our cities and towns across this vast land. We all have heard the depressing statistics concerning teen pregnancies, divorce, single parents, drugs, crime, and immorality.

I remember sitting in front of my TV set years ago, watching the news reports on the LA riots, wondering, "How much worse do things have to get before we Christians get serious in our prayers?" Then when students began killing other students in our public schools I found myself asking, "When will the church wake up?" The constant problems we face in this country—not to mention what's happening around the world—should give us strong reason to be wary about the future.

If you are not concerned about what's happening in America and how it affects your family, then I'd compare you to an ostrich that sticks his head in a hole and thinks he's safe while a nearby lion is stalking him.

America is in trouble.

We have turned our backs on God in almost every institution in our nation.

America's only hope is if God's people will make a commitment to righteous living and humbly intercede for our nation. Then, our country could radically change.

> *[If] my people who are called by My name humble them-*
> *selves and pray and seek my face and turn from their*
> *wicked ways, then I will hear from heaven, will forgive*
> *their sin and will heal their land.*
>
> (2 Chronicles 7:14)

Let me ask you once again: Do you believe in prayer?

Do you believe that the prayer of the righteous is powerful and effective? (James 5:16)

Do you believe that if we pray, God will heal our land?

Do you believe God rescues and delivers those who pray? (Psalm 34)

Do you really believe that God answers prayer? The Bible says He does! (Psalm 65:2-5) These questions are the most important you and I could ever ask ourselves.

BELIEF BREEDS PRAYER

About fifteen years ago, I asked our Lord for several weeks: "Why is it that so few people come to the church prayer meetings? Why do only a few of Your people have a quiet time every day with You? Why isn't prayer a bigger priority in our lives?"

I believe the Lord spoke to me and said, "My people do not pray because My people do not believe Me!"

This answer may seem too simplistic, but I urge you to give it some honest thought. If you knew of a doctor who had developed a pill that would ensure safety from a plague that was destroying the people of your city, wouldn't you immediately buy a supply of those pills? If the directions for these pills said, "Take one every single day," wouldn't you make sure the pills were taken each and every day? I cannot imagine ever skipping a day, let alone a week or more at a time. If you are like me, you'd take these life-saving pills each day, knowing and believing that they would keep you from getting the deadly plague.

My friend, we Christians have trouble with prayer because we really do not believe that prayer is going to make a big enough difference in our circumstances—in our jobs, our marriages, our relationships, our city and country. If we really believed prayer would make a difference, we'd all be praying much more than we are presently.

In November 1994, we had many righteous individuals elected to public office on the local, state, and national levels. Many were saying that we had turned a corner; America was waking up, revival was coming. At that time my fear was that Christians would grow even more complacent thinking the battle for America was almost won and the need for prevailing prayer was diminished.

Such is NOT the case!

Our country continues to decay, and the deterioration will progress until God's people take responsibility and believe God for a miracle. There is only one hope for America and it isn't the Tea Party, any politician or program.

Our only hope is our Savior, Jesus Christ.

The problem with America resides in the heart of man, and only Jesus can change a heart. Friend, we need a powerful revival, an awakening, a renewal in America or we will soon go the way of Roman Empire and other decadent civilizations that no longer exist.

Throughout the Bible, God has made it perfectly clear that if any nation corrupts itself and becomes hopelessly wicked, He will make that nation desolate.

> *I will make the land a desolation and a waste, and the pride of her power will cease; and the mountains of Israel will be desolate so that no one will pass through. Then they will know that I am the Lord, when I make the land a desolation and a waste because of all their abominations which they have committed.*
>
> (Ezekiel 33:28-29)

How to Win When Hopelessly Helpless

In 2 Chronicles 20, there is a story about Jehoshaphat, King of Judah, and the crisis his small nation faced. I believe God's people can profit by reviewing how this ancient nation handled what seemed to be a hopeless circumstance. Here's the situation: Judah was being invaded from the south by a large coalition of forces. Judah's army was hopelessly outnumbered; defeat seemed inevitable.

> *Now it came about that the sons of Moab and the sons of Ammon together with the sons of the Meunites came to make war against Jehoshaphat. Then some came and reported to Jehoshaphat saying, "A great multitude is coming against you from beyond the sea, out of the Aram and behold, they are in Hazazon-tamar (that is Engedi)." Jehoshaphat was afraid and turned his attention to seek the Lord, and proclaimed a fast throughout all Judah.*
>
> (2 Chronicles 20:1–3)

I love these verses because most of us can easily relate to them. When situations enter our lives that seem overwhelming, that could have serious consequences, it shakes us up. We get anxious, lose sleep, feel threatened, and too often we become consumed with worry.

When I watch the rulings of our judicial system in America, I become concerned.

When I take a hard look at our educational system, I become alarmed.

When confronted with the influence of the media, I'm angered.

When looking at what our government has become, I'm ashamed.

When thinking about the kind of world my children will grow up in, I'm fearful.

When you and I, as Christians, find ourselves faced with predicaments and circumstances that seem overwhelming, we have three choices.

1. Denial

Like the ostrich, we can stick our heads in the sand and pretend there is no danger. After the initial shock, we set the issue aside and go ahead with our lives as if everything is all right. We probably hope that someone else will do something about the problem or that it will just go away. The problem seems too big for us—so we ignore it. "How can I possibly do anything about this problem? I'm only one person." Many Christians (I believe the number is decreasing, praise the Lord) have simply refused to come to terms with reality. As long as nothing affects their immediate world, they do nothing. Because everything seems to be going well in their small circle of life, what happens "over there" does not concern them.

Often I see men and women go about their lives in what seems to be an apparent denial that they are facing major problems. In the midst of this denial, their marriage falls apart, their homes go into foreclosure, their children become more and more rebellious—yet they just continue to try to tune out all the unpleasant things.

2. Our Own Efforts

When confronted with overwhelming circumstances we can try to work things out ourselves, relying on our own efforts and abilities.

How many times have we all tried to manipulate people and circumstances in an attempt to take control of a situation? Without seeking God in these situations, they result in a constant obsession with problems, and end up ultimately causing total frustration and defeat.

3. Trust in God

The right choice was demonstrated by Jehoshaphat. He faced the overwhelming situation realizing that with God's help, he would be able to have the victory or overcome it (2 Chronicles 20:3). Do what godly men and women have been doing for thousands of years with great results. Take your problems to the Lord in prayer!

Jehoshaphat realized he needed a miracle, and miracles are what God does best.

AMERICA'S BATTLE IS THE LORD'S

Dear Reader, we desperately need miracles for our country, our cities, our churches, families, even our own lives. God's Word clearly demonstrates that miracles happen when His people humble themselves, pour out their hearts to Him, and then trust Him to intervene.

God responds to those who put their trust in Him.

Humble yourselves in the presence of the Lord, and He will exalt you.

(James 4:10)

Therefore humble yourselves therefore under the mighty hand of God, that He may exalt you at the proper time, casting all your anxiety on Him, because He cares for you.

(1 Peter 5:6-7)

I sought the Lord, and He answered me and delivered me from all my fears. The angel of the Lord encamps around those who fear Him, and rescues them. The righteous cry, and the Lord hears and delivers them out of all their troubles. Many are the afflictions of the righteous, but the Lord delivers him out of them all.

(Psalm 34:4, 7, 17, 19)

These are only a few of the multitude of scriptures that declare the Lord's response to the prayerful requests we place humbly before Him.

2 Chronicles 20:4 says,

So Judah gathered together to seek help from the Lord; they even came from all the cities of Judah to seek the Lord.

Do you see it?

They had a giant prayer meeting.

In verses 5-11, we have an account of the prayer King Jehoshaphat offered to God before all the people. Then, in verse 12, he says,

We are powerless before this great multitude who are coming against us; nor do we know what to do, but our eyes are on You.

In verses 14-15, we read:

> *Then in the midst of the assembly the Spirit of the*
> *Lord came upon Jahaziel the son of Zechariah, the*
> *son of Benaiah, the son of Jeiel, the son of Mattaniah,*
> *the Levite of the sons of Asaph; and he said, "Listen,*
> *all Judah and the inhabitants of Jerusalem and King*
> *Jehoshaphat: thus says the Lord to you, 'Do not fear*
> *or be dismayed because of this great multitude, for the*
> *battle is not yours, but God's.'"*

This is one of the most important and powerful scriptures in the Bible; underline it and memorize it.

The battle for our children, for education, for morality, for good government is not solely ours but the Lord's.

The battles in your personal life are not yours—but the Lord's.

The battle for America, our communities and families is the Lord's.

This key biblical principle is illustrated again in Deuteronomy 3:22.

> *Do not fear them, for the Lord your God is the one*
> *fighting for you.*

PRACTICAL INTERCESSION

We must always remind ourselves that we are first fighting a spiritual battle, not only in our society but also in our personal situations. Our first assignment in this battle is intercession and prayer.

Yes, we need to be involved in the political process, in evangelism, in feeding the poor, in going to counseling. These are all logical steps we can take to be the salt of the earth and seek His Kingdom first. But without prayer, without first recognizing our dependency for victory in Jesus Christ, we are ultimately doomed to failure.

Why?

Because our efforts become a work of the flesh, obtaining little lasting fruit.

> *A man can receive nothing unless it has been given him from heaven.*

(John 3:27)

Prayer is important because it releases God's possibilities into our impossibilities. When God's supernatural power is released into personal situations or national circumstances, miracles can and will happen. Let me give you an example.

When our church grew to a size where we needed to have our own facilities (we had been renting a recreation center on Sunday mornings), we began looking to lease property. In San Diego's East County, this is not an easy proposition. It seemed that no one wanted to have a church in "their" neighborhood. Another problem: to rent a building we had to obtain a "Conditional Use Permit," a process that takes many months (often much longer). During this waiting period, no improvements or meetings can take place in the facility. As you can imagine, very few building owners want to take their property off the market for at least three months while this whole process unfolds.

After much searching, we finally located a Christian businessman who owned considerable commercial and industrial space in our city. He agreed to hold 8,500 square feet while we worked with the city. But, he warned, "I have personally tried very hard to get several other churches in my buildings. I've written letters, met with City Council members, spoke at planning commission meetings, but we have always been denied. As far as I'm concerned, if you get this permit it would be tantamount to Jesus walking on the water."

After that speech, we did not proceed with a great deal of hope, but since this was the only building in two years that had been made available to us, we had no other choice. We filed all the necessary paperwork, wrote letters to all the planning commissioners, and waited for our hearing date in front of the planning commission. As the day of our hearing approached, it became abundantly clear that the majority of the planning commission felt that "A church did not belong in an industrial zone. Available industrial space is far too valuable to the city to let a church occupy it."

During the days leading up to our hearing before the Planning Commission, our little church united in prayer for a miracle. The night of the hearing, we scheduled a prayer meeting in a small church that was made available to us about one block from City Hall. The prayer meeting started at 7:00 p.m. and was scheduled to run until the Commission had voted on our request. We only had three representatives from our church at the meeting: my brother, Mark (co-pastor of our church), our real estate agent, and me.

The day of the meeting we learned from a good friend of the chairman of the Planning Commission that there was "no way" the commission would give us a permit.

We did not have the votes.

When our time came to speak, both Mark and I presented our case. Frankly, we came off quite poorly, as did our Real Estate Agent. After many questions directed at Mark and me, and closing statements from most of the commission on why they couldn't vote for our request, the commission took their vote.

Meanwhile, our prayer meeting continued.

Because of the close proximity to City Hall, those praying were continually getting updates on how things were going. The final update they received was that "It doesn't look good. The Commission is about ready to take a vote."

Well, vote they did… and we won—four to one.

You could have heard a pin drop in that chamber.

No one—and I mean no one—expected this result. There was complete silence, seemingly forever. Finally, someone in authority said, "The request passes four to one."

I couldn't believe it! We had just witnessed a miracle!

The majority of the Planning Commission were not professing Christians, and just moments before they had told us why they couldn't vote for our request.

To this day I believe two or three of those commissioners went home and told their spouses, "I really don't know why I voted for that church's request. I just did."

That moment changed my outlook on prayer forever. I learned that prayer does cause the impossible to happen. Prayer is the key to unlock that which the Church is seeking in our country—revival in our churches and one nation under God. God will push back the enemy before us if we are willing to pray.

PRAYER ALLOWS GOD TO ACT

Let's go back to 2 Chronicles 20 and see how God responded to a people committed to prayer. The Lord instructed the nation of Judah to go out against the great multitude that had gathered against them and not to fear or be dismayed because He was with them. As the tiny nation of Judah went out to confront their enemies, singing praises to God, this is what happened:

The Lord set ambushes against the sons of Ammon, Moab and Mount Seir, who had come against Judah; so they were routed. For the sons of Ammon and Moab rose up against the inhabitants of Mount Seir destroying them completely; and when they had finished with the inhabitants of Seir, they helped to destroy one another. When Judah came to the lookout of the wilderness, they looked toward the multitude, and behold, they were corpses lying on the ground, and no one had escaped. When Jehoshaphat and his people came to take their spoil, they found much among them... And they were three days taking the spoil because there was so much.

(2 Chronicles 20:22-25)

Isn't this a great story? I love it because it fills me with hope as I remember that the Bible says that the Lord does not change (Malachi 3:6). Therefore, if we pray and wait on God, He will act—He will answer us, giving us strategies and miracles.

Now, let us go back to the original question I asked at the beginning of this chapter. Do you believe in prayer?

If your answer is yes, do your actions coincide with what you say you believe?

Some years ago a 16-year-old Christian girl was brutally murdered in a quiet residential area near our church. Everyone was asking "Why?" The media was asking, "Why?" Family and friends all asked, "Why?" At the funeral, her pastor asked, "Why did God let this happen?"

I wanted to scream, "I know why! We live in an evil and perverse generation that is getting worse all the time. This young girl was a casualty!"

I'm sure you know of many similar situations in your own community that concern you deeply. You're probably concerned and troubled about circumstances in your family, church, work, school, etc.

The real question is:

What are you going to do about it?

There is only one answer, and the Bible has it. When God's people pray, He acts and heals their land (2 Chronicles 7:14).

CHAPTER THREE

Prayer Changes Things

Have you ever wondered why the Lord was so careful to give us a written account of the early Church? Was it simply as a record, a history of the spread of Christianity that would give us a sense of connection with the past? Was it just a detailed account of a special Apostolic period when God moved in miraculous ways—ways He would never move in again? Did God want us to remember the beginnings of the Church in the same manner that the Jews were to remember their deliverance from Egypt?

When I read the book of Acts, I find myself saying, "If only these things could happen in our church, our city, our nation today!" The book of Acts fills me with a great desire to see God's supernatural power manifested in our own time.

If the book of Acts is really nothing more than a history book (as some theologians teach), then it seems to me that God would be very cruel to create a desire in us to see the same move of the Holy Spirit today—a move that supposedly could never be fulfilled.

But, I believe this "historical" theology is too narrow, and it misses a key purpose for the book of Acts.

David tells us in Psalm 145:19,

*He will fulfill the desire of those who fear Him; He will
also hear their cry.*

In Psalm 37:4, he says:

*Delight yourself in the Lord; and He will give you the
desires of your heart.*

Our Heavenly Father would never create a desire that He could not
totally satisfy. One of my favorite passages in the Bible says that when
we seek God and His Kingdom, we will never be disappointed (Romans
10:11). Isaiah 28:16 (NIV) said it first:

The one who trusts [in Him] will never be dismayed.

Obviously the book of Acts is a history book, but God also gave it
to us to create a hunger, a desire to see His Spirit being poured out in
our day. The book of Acts is a book of hope for what can be, of what
is possible in every generation. We serve a God Who is *"the same
yesterday and today and forever"* (Hebrews 13:8).

For I, the Lord, do not change.

(Malachi 3:6)

We can have confidence that our Lord deals with His people the
same today as He did in the early Church. We have the same basic
emotional and spiritual needs as the early Christians.

When we understand that God remains constant throughout the
ages, it births great hope in us of what is possible in our situation,
our family, church, city, and nation. The Bible tells us that when God
births a hope in our hearts, it is a *"hope* [that] *does not disappoint"*
(Romans 5:5).

HOPE FOR ALL CIRCUMSTANCES

In Acts 12 the Jerusalem Church faced a desperate situation. Herod and the Jews were determined to destroy this new religious sect. The story of what happened, and how the plans of Herod and the Jews were thwarted by prayer, gives us great hope for our own situations and circumstances.

> *Now about that time Herod the king laid hands on some who belonged to the church in order to mistreat them. And he had James the brother of John put to death with a sword. When he saw that it pleased the Jews, he proceeded to arrest Peter also. Now it was during the days of Unleavened Bread. When he had seized him, he put him in prison, delivering him to four squads of soldiers to guard him, intending after the Passover to bring him out before the people. So Peter was kept in the prison, but prayer for him was being made fervently by the church to God.*

(Acts 12:1–5)

Because of this prayer, God sent an angel who miraculously released Peter from Prison. When Peter realized he was not dreaming…

> *…he went to the house of Mary, the mother of John who was also called Mark, where many were gathered together and were praying. When he knocked at the door of the gate, a servant-girl named Rhoda came to answer. When she recognized Peter's voice, because of her joy she did not open the gate, but ran in and announced that Peter was standing in front of the gate. They said to her, "You are out of your mind!" But she kept insisting that it was so. They kept saying, "It is his angel." But*

Peter continued knocking; and when they had opened the door, they saw him and were amazed.

(Acts 12:12–16)

There are several valuable lessons in this passage we need to learn to overcome desperate circumstances in our own lives, our families, churches, communities, and world. Keep in mind that what worked for the Jerusalem Church will work for us today—that is why the Holy Spirit recorded it for us.

PRAYER: THE FIRST OPTION

<u>The First Valuable Lesson</u> is that our first reaction to any circumstance or desperate situation must be prayer.

The Apostle Peter's sentence already had been determined—he was going to be executed! No one in the Jerusalem Church doubted this, especially considering what had already happened to the apostle James. Facing this critical situation, the Church set their hearts toward prayer. In verse five we are told they "prayed fervently," asking God to intervene and supernaturally thwart the plans of Herod and the Jews.

Dear Reader, prayer is the real battleground of our world. Events of history, changed lives, loved ones saved, marriages restored, the impossible becoming possible—all have been brought about by the followers of Jesus praying fervently.

The Jerusalem Church had one great weapon (intercessory prayer) to use in combating the enormous power of King Herod, who held the power of life and death over his subjects. The satanic pawn, King Herod, was no match for the power released when the early Christians prayed.

Do not be deceived.

You and I have the same power available to us today when we pray against the godless circumstances constantly confronting our families, churches, communities, and nation. Here in California in 2008 we had a ballot proposition that would require our state constitution to define marriage between a man and woman. We all knew that without a miracle, this Proposition 8 would not pass. Churches across California went on a 40-day fast, praying for a miracle. When we started praying and fasting the polls didn't look good: 38% in favor and 55% opposing. Forty days later Proposition 8 passed 52.3% to 47.7%. It was a miracle and it sent shock waves across America.

The one great determining factor of our success or failure in all areas of our lives is prayer.

The Church's success in reaching young people, influencing our city, and in all ministry is always determined by prayer.

Why?

Because prayer opens the doors of Heaven.

Prayer ushers us into the presence of God.

Prayer is the channel through which all good things flow from God to His people. If you want God's supernatural power working in your life, then you must be a man or woman of prayer.

To accomplish great things for God, to change circumstances or counter godless pressures, we must understand that the battle is first won in the spiritual realm on our knees. Then the results are seen in the physical realm. Remember, Paul said,

> *Our struggle is not against flesh and blood, but… against spiritual forces… in the heavenly places.*
>
> (Ephesians 6:12)

My friend, we all need divine help to live in this world, raise children, make decisions, experience fulfilling marriages, love unselfishly, be obedient, overcome bondages, have victory over difficult situations, and live holy lives. When we do not pray, the supernatural is left out of our daily lives. James 4:2 says it best: "*You do not have because you do not ask.*"

Prayer Power Stronger than Plagues

The power that raised Jesus from the dead dwells in all believers (Romans 8:11) and is released in part through our prayers. Christians become weak, feeble, depressed, defeated, overwhelmed, and misguided all because of their failure to pray. Remember what the Apostle Paul said in Philippians 4:6-7.

> *Be anxious for nothing, but in everything by prayer and supplication with thanksgiving let your requests be made known to God. And the peace of God, which surpasses all comprehension, will guard your hearts and your minds in Christ Jesus.*

When we fail to pray, God's power is surely lacking in our lives. Therefore, we have no power; we become depressed and defeated. But when we look to God in prayer and lean not on our own understanding, God's peace, His love, and supernatural anointing are made available to us.

In the 1800s a grasshopper plague came upon the state of Minnesota while "Honest John" Pillsbury was governor. A similar plague the year before had devastated all the crops. Therefore, by the second year, the whole state's economy was in jeopardy. Dr. R. A. Torrey tells how the plague was prevented:

A number of influential men from various States met in consultation as to the best means of ridding them of the plague. The Governor of a neighboring state urged that the only thing to be done to escape the threatening plague was to appoint a day of prayer wherein all praying people should unite in praying to God to remove the grasshoppers. John S. Pillsbury accepted the suggestion, returned home to St. Paul, and issued a proclamation that all people who believed in a God that answered prayer should proceed on a given day to their places of worship and pray to God to remove the grasshoppers from Minnesota. On the appointed day a wonderful thing occurred. In some places the grasshoppers died by the millions in the trenches; those that were able to fly rose up and flew out of the state of Minnesota. A few lingered on, but they too, eventually disappeared, and the crops were saved. There has never been a grasshopper plague in Minnesota from that day to this, though there have been plagues in other states.[1]

Was this a coincidence?

I doubt it. I like the old saying, "When I pray coincidences happen; when I fail to pray, coincidences do not seem to happen."

Some time ago, a couple from our church was concerned about their teenage daughter who was saying and doing ungodly things. The couple decided to immerse their daughter in prayer, petitioning God to stop her rebellion and remove the worldly influences in her life. Sometime later, their daughter decided to make dramatic changes in her life, giving herself over to God's ways.

Coincidental?

---

[1] Davis, George T.B. Torrey and Alexander: *The Story of a World-Wide Revival.* (Fleming H. Revell Co., 1905), p. 154.

No way.

One of my favorite biblical examples of seeking the Lord first when confronted with difficult situations is King David. Listen to his words:

> *O God of my praise, Do not be silent! For they have opened the wicked and deceitful mouth against me; they have spoken against me with a lying tongue. They have also surrounded me with words of hatred, and fought against me without cause. In return for my love they act as my accusers; but I am in prayer.*
>
> (Psalms 109:1-4)

In the face of adversity, David is in prayer. David realized that when his circumstances were bad, he had hope. He could go to God in prayer. His past experiences had shown him that prayer released God's power into situations, changing things.

> *Now I know that the Lord saves His anointed; He will answer him from His holy heaven with the saving strength of His right hand. Some boast in chariots and some in horses, but we will boast in the name of the Lord, our God.*
>
> (Psalms 20:6-7)

David learned that God did answer his prayers. He had come to realize God's strength and power were released into all circumstances where he trusted and prayed.

Our first reaction to desperate situations or the frustrations of daily life must be prayer—it releases God's power and possibilities into our world.

GOD WILL ACT ON YOUR PRAYER

The Second Valuable Lesson is that God acts on our behalf as we wait on Him.

As the Jerusalem Church prayed, great things started to happen. Of course, they could not see anything happening. The circumstances looked totally hopeless, but God was working.

When we pray, God acts; things happen whether we see them or not.

I believe we have not seen a greater demonstration of God's power in our lives, churches, and country because we have been a people of little prayer. Hopefully, this is beginning to change. Christians all across America and the world are falling on their knees, humbling themselves before God and asking for revival, evangelism, changed hearts, and justice.

God will hear and act on our prayers.

> *Call to Me and I will answer you…*
>
> (Jeremiah 33:3)

As you and I pray and put our trust in God, He goes to work in our circumstances about which we are deeply concerned. The Bible says God acts while we wait for Him.

> *For from days of old they have not heard or perceived by ear, nor has the eye seen a God besides You, Who acts on behalf of the one who waits for Him.*
>
> (Isaiah 64:4)

Prayer releases God's resurrected power into our lives, churches, communities, nation, and world. As we pray, God literally goes to work on our behalf. As E. M. Bounds said, "Prayer puts God to work."

If you are praying, God is acting on your behalf even as you read this. Your prayers have literally released Him into your situation. If you are praying, your circumstances, your church, your city will change.

Just keep on praying.

GOD ANSWERS, INFLUENCING OUR LIVES

The Third Valuable Lesson is that when you pray, expect God to answer.

The Jerusalem Church gives us a vivid illustration of the fact that many Christians do not really believe that God can or will answer their prayers. If the Jerusalem believers had been praying with expectation, they would have run to open the gate when the servant girl announced that Peter was standing in front of it. They were praying, which is the proper response to crisis, but they must not have believed God would really do anything.

When we pray, we must pray expecting God to answer us.

> *But as for me, I will watch expectantly for the Lord; I will wait for the God of my salvation. My God will hear me. Do not rejoice over me, O my enemy. though I fall I will rise; though I dwell in darkness, the Lord is a light for me... He will bring me out to the light, and I will see His righteousness.*
>
> (Micah 7:7-9)

In the book of Psalms, King David writes how he had experienced God's answers to his prayers.

> *O You who hear prayer, to You all men come... By awesome deeds You answer us in righteousness, O God of our salvation.*
>
> (Psalm 65:2, 5)

You may be praying for something right now that as of yet has not been fulfilled.

Keep praying.

Keep expecting God to answer.

He always does.

Friend, as we pray we must expect God to answer because He promised that He would, and God does not lie. God said He will answer prayer, so He will.

> *If you abide in Me, and My words abide in you, ask whatever you wish, and it will be done for you. My Father is glorified by this, that you bear much fruit, and so prove to be My disciples.*
>
> (John 15:7-8)

If we continue to pray, it will bring God's influence to bear on the people, circumstances and concerns we have brought before the Lord. If you and I commit ourselves to developing a prayer life, it will bring God's influence into our lives and hasten revival.

Why?

Because when we pray and seek God's face, He begins to change and transform us (2 Corinthians 3:18). When we start to pray consistently, our prayers slowly change. Where once we were only concerned with self, our prayers begin to reflect the heart of God. As we increasingly pray, God begins to give us His burdens for the world and especially that His Church would be revived.

God has given our church, Foothills Christian Church, an awesome vision for ministering to San Diego's East County. As we have prayed, the Lord has expanded and clarified our ministry and our assignment in San Diego.

The Foothills Experience

In 1990, Foothills Christian Church was small, with an approximate attendance of 150 on Sunday mornings. As we prayed, our Lord gave us a vision for reaching 1,000 youth and children each week. Not long after that vision, we had a full-time youth and children's pastor, plus countless volunteers.

At this writing, we have surpassed this goal and are reaching 5,000-6,000 youth and children in total attendance each week!

We began to pray about marriages, asking God to miraculously restore countless couples. It was not long after these prayers that we had written our own 10-week marriage enrichment course, and we saw God raise up an anointed couple to oversee this ministry. The Lord also sent us gifted and qualified biblical counselors to help in this area.

We began praying about people who were in bondage to alcohol, drugs, homosexuality, and various other types of abuses.

Guess what?

God brought a couple out of nowhere who with our help founded a 12-acre ranch for those who want deliverance from these assorted bondages.

We had a vision for a youth center for unchurched, troubled kids.

You guessed it.

Our fourth Youth Venture Club now ministers and disciples hundreds of youth each week. The City Council of El Cajon and the Board of Supervisors of San Diego gave us special awards for the center's work with youth. We prayed about starting an elementary school, Jr. High school, and finally a high school. God has miraculously provided the resources for all. We prayed about starting Bible Clubs in public schools in East County. At present we have after- school Bible Clubs in 28 public schools.

These ministries are only a fraction of all the new outreaches that have started in our church in the last twelve years, and all are the direct result of prayer.

My brother Mark and I have been co-pastoring this church for twenty-five years. The first five we worked very hard, but not much happened. It was only after we deeply committed ourselves to prayer that things began to really move.

Prayer does change things.

In another chapter of this book I will share with you about our church Prayer Society. These prayer warriors have brought a spiritual dynamic to our church's ministry unlike anything we've ever seen before. We believe this ministry is the most important in the church. Prayer primes, pushes, and supernaturally anoints all our ministries.

PRAY FOR DIVINE INTERVENTION

If you are discouraged or depressed concerning events in your life, commit them to the Lord in prayer; put God to work in that situation and expect things to change.

When Paul and Silas were ministering in the city of Philippa, they encountered severe opposition. They were beaten with rods, thrown down into the deepest part of the prison, and had their feet put into stocks.

Things were not going too well. Let's pick up the story in Acts 16, starting at verse 25:

> *But about midnight Paul and Silas were praying and singing hymns of praise to God, and the prisoners were listening to them; and suddenly there came a great earthquake, so that the foundations of the prison house were shaken; and immediately all the doors were opened and everyone's chains were unfastened. When the jailer awoke and saw the prison doors opened, he drew his sword and was about to kill himself, supposing that the prisoners had escaped. But Paul cried out with a loud voice, saying, "Do not harm yourself, for we are all here!" And he called for lights and rushed in, and trembling with fear he fell down before Paul and Silas, and after he brought them out, he said, "Sirs, what must I do to be saved?" They said, "Believe in the Lord Jesus, and you will be saved, you and your household." And they spoke the word of the Lord to him together with all who were in his house. And he took them that very hour of the night and washed their wounds, and immediately he was baptized, he and all his household. And he brought them into his house and set food before them, and rejoiced greatly, having believed in God with his whole household.*

Paul had learned over the years that prayer really did change things. So in that dark hour, he and Silas began to pray, and God intervened.

Coincidence?

Try to tell that to the jailer. It is obvious that the earthquake and what followed were a direct result of their prayers. The Lord promised to answer our prayers, and He will. It really is that simple.

The Bible says we have a God who cannot lie (Hebrews 6:18; Titus 1:2). So, unless we want to call God a liar, understand that He will answer our prayers.

In James 5:16 we read:

> *The effective prayer of a righteous man can accomplish much.*

We can accomplish much through our persistent intercession before God. We can change our unwanted situations if we look to God in prayer for wisdom and deliverance.

Humble prayer, prayer according to God's will (1 John 5:14–15), puts God to work and releases His power, authority, and anointing.

Prayer changes things.

So start praying!

CHAPTER FOUR

Persevering in Prayer

Most of you reading this book would agree that we who live in the twenty-first century live very busy lives. We like and expect quick results: instant coffee, instant oatmeal, Eggo Waffles, ATMs, drive-through banks, quick car repairs, microwaves, etc. Unfortunately, we often evaluate service solely by how quickly it was accomplished.

Is it any wonder that we have gravitated towards teachings on prayer that promise quick results? We readily accept those who teach doctrines such as, "If you pray using this formula, your prayers will be answered quickly."

One of the lessons I have learned about God over the years is that God is never in a hurry. We may be in a hurry but He never is.

If we truly want our prayers to accomplish much, to release revival in individuals, churches, and communities, then we must understand the principle of perseverance and persistent prayer. The dictionary defines a persistent person as someone who "continues firmly on some course... insistent as in repeating or continuing an action." This definition describes a person who never gives up, who just keeps doing the right thing no matter how tough or inconvenient. Jesus was very specific in telling us that this type of person pleases God, especially where prayer is concerned.

In Luke 11, Jesus' disciples, knowing that the secret of Jesus' ministry was prayer, asked Him to teach them how to pray. Jesus then gave His disciples a simple prayer outline, which later became known as the Lord's Prayer.

Immediately afterward, Jesus gave His disciples important instructions concerning prayer, explaining the significance of persevering until the answer comes or the promise is fulfilled.

Jesus knew that there would be struggles and trials not only for His disciples but for all who would follow after them. He wanted to be sure they understood that persistence and perseverance in prayer will always gain the victory.

ASK AND IT SHALL BE OPENED

Then He said to them, "Suppose one of you has a friend, and goes to him at midnight and says to him, 'Friend, lend me three loaves; for a friend of mine has come to me from a journey, and I have nothing to set before him'; and from inside he answers and says, 'Do not bother me; the door has already been shut and my children and I are in bed; I cannot get up and give you anything.' I tell you, even though he will not get up and give him anything because he is his friend, yet because of his persistence he will get up and give him as much as he needs. So I say to you, ask, and it will be given to you; seek and you will find; knock, and it will be opened to you. For everyone who asks, receives; and he who seeks, finds; and to him who knocks, it will be opened.

(Luke 11: 5–10)

Jesus shared this parable to illustrate that if persistence can get a man out of bed in the middle of the night, can we not count on God to answer our persistent prayers?

This brings up an important question. Do we have to persuade, harangue, or pester God until He answers us?

Is prayer simply bugging God until He relents and says, "Okay, you can have what you ask?"

Does God have to be coaxed?

Is prayer a means of twisting God's arm to extort a blessing?

Of course not!

I confess there have been instances in my life where I tried to pester and manipulate God to come around to my way of thinking. I prayed, fasted and prayed some more, but I did not receive what I was asking. Why?

Because I was asking with wrong motives.

Here's how James 4:3 explains it:

> *You ask and do not receive, because you ask with wrong motives, so that you may spend it on your pleasures.*

I was praying outside of the will of God for my life, so God was not going to answer my prayer the way I desired. He had something better planned for my life.

Praise the Lord! We serve a wonderful God!

I thank Him for not giving me those things that are not in His will for my life. Don't you?

On the other hand, when we pray according to the will of God and persevere in prayer, God will always answer us.

> *This is the confidence which we have before Him, that,*
> *if we ask anything according to His will, He hears us.*
> *And if we know that He hears us in whatever we ask, we*
> *know that we have the requests which we have asked*
> *from Him.*
>
> (1 John 5: 14–15)

George Mueller said "When I am convinced that a thing is right and for the glory of God, I go on praying for it until the answer comes... I never give up!"

When Jesus told us to ask, seek, and knock, grammatically it is a continuous action—we are to keep asking, keep seeking, keep knocking until the answer comes. Jesus uses a parable to help us see that if persistence can get a man out of bed because of his friends repeated asking, we can count on our heavenly Father to hear and answer our prayers.

GOD'S WILL

Some of you are probably thinking, "This sounds great, Dave, but how do I know that I'm praying according to God's will?"

Look at God's Word.

We should always examine our prayers to see if they line up with the Bible. For example, if I am praying for an unsaved relative, I know this is the will of God because He...

> *...desires all men to be saved and to come to the*
> *knowledge of the truth.*
>
> (1 Timothy 2:4)

It is often asked, "When I pray for physical healing, how do I know this is God's will?" I'm going to spend time on this subject in a latter chapter, but doesn't the Bible specifically command us to pray for the sick? (James 5:13–15)

The main reason we see so few miraculous healings is a direct result of our lack of faith in obeying the command to pray for the sick.

I believe it is crucial that we continue to pray for healing until the Lord sends healing, an explanation, or takes the saint home. The Word of God tells us that our Heavenly Father always answers us and always answers in a positive way. (In a later chapter I will explain why I believe God always answers in a positive way and how this revelation literally revolutionized my prayer life.)

There are some things we pray for that are not directly addressed in Scripture. How do we know God's will in these matters? I have found that if I persist in praying, God literally changes and transforms my thoughts to parallel His. So just keep on praying, and God will change your prayers to coincide with His. The end result will be that you are praying according to God's will.

The boldness to persist, to keep asking, to keep seeking and knocking is derived from Scripture. Ephesians 3:12 tells us,

> *We have boldness and confident access through faith in Him.*

Hebrews 10:19 says,

> *Therefore, brethren... we have confidence to enter the holy place by the blood of Jesus.*

Many other scriptures remind us of our ability through Christ to come boldly before God (Ephesians 2:18, Hebrews 4:16). It seems obvious to me that God is pleased when we persist in prayer.

It is my belief that God wants us to be active participants in His kingdom. Somehow, our prayers help the purposes of God. Someone said it this way: "Our prayers move the hand of God."

NEVER GIVE UP ON PRAYER

You and I are weapons of the Lord Jesus Christ. We are part of His arsenal. Our prayers somehow release His power into the earth to bring down strongholds, to deliver people from demonic bondages, and to heal the sick. I'll be the first to admit that I don't know why He needs or even desires our help, but this surely is His plan.

Let us look at yet another passage where Jesus teaches us about persevering in prayer:

> *Now He was telling them a parable to show that at all times they ought to pray and not lose heart, saying, "In a certain city there was a judge who did not fear God, and did not respect man. There was a widow in that city, and she kept coming to him, saying, 'Give me legal protection from my opponent.' For a while he was unwilling; but afterward he said to himself, 'Even though I do not fear God nor respect man, yet because this widow bothers me, I will give her legal protection, otherwise by continually coming she will wear me out.'" And the Lord said, "Hear what the unrighteous judge said; now, will not God bring about justice for His elect who cry to Him day and night, and will He delay long over them?"*

(Luke 18:1–7)

Here Jesus teaches us about persistent prayer by contrast. If an ungenerous judge grants a widow's request because of her perseverance, how much more will our Heavenly Father answer our prayers?

The Lord Jesus told this parable so that whenever it was read or shared, His people would forever know His will on persistent prayer. Jesus is encouraging us to persist in prayer. The answer, solution, or remedy will come if we but trust Him.

I'm convinced that too often we miss a blessing from God simply because we give up in our intercessory prayer.

We live in an age of quitters. When the going gets tough, people quit. We walk away from marriages, jobs, and various other responsibilities because we simply do not want to stick it out.

God doesn't want disciples who run at the first sign of adversity. He's looking for men and women who will endure the hard times through to victory. Too many Christians give up before God's answer before the victory—comes. Many actually use God as their excuse for not continuing in prayer, piously exclaiming, "It must be the will of God." Most of the time this remark is nothing more than a lie to cover up spiritual laziness. The worst part of this lie is that they end up missing out on the victory God has planned for them.

Do you want to miss out on anything that God has planned for you?

I hope not!

Again, in Luke 18:1 we read, *"Now He was telling them a parable to show them that at all times they ought to pray and not lose heart."* Jesus is telling us to always pray and not give up, but doesn't He also communicate that we might give up if we don't continue to pray?

All translations of this verse give the same idea. Either we pray or we despair, lose heart, or give up. The Greek word "lose heart" (*ekkacheho*) can be translated: "To faint, to be weak, be discouraged, be timid, give up, lack courage." This Greek word is important because in all of Jesus parables there are comparisons and contrasts and this parable is no exception. There are only two positions. Either you pray or you give up. You pray or you will become discouraged, timid, defeated, weak, or lack distinctiveness.

We pray and involve our lives in a relationship with Jesus Christ or we lack. We pray or what we attempt is done weakly and has little distinctiveness.

But if we pray we "*will mount up with wings like eagles... run and not get tired... walk and not become weary.*"(Isaiah 40:31)

Friend, if you're still reading this book you obviously want the kind of life Isaiah described. Most people interested in prayer are hungry for God's blessing in their own lives as well as the world around them.

In Matthew 15:22–28 we read:

> *And a Canaanite woman from that region came out and began to cry out, saying, "Have mercy on me, Lord, Son of David; my daughter is cruelly demon-possessed." But He did not answer her a word. And His disciples came and implored Him, saying, "Send her away, because she keeps shouting at us." But He answered and said, "I was sent only to the lost sheep of the house of Israel." But she came and began to bow down before Him, saying, "Lord, help me!" And He answered and said, "It is not good to take the children's bread and throw it to the dogs." But she said, "Yes, Lord; but even the dogs feed on the crumbs which fall from their masters' table." Then Jesus said to her, "O woman, your faith is great; it shall be done for you as you wish." And her daughter was healed at once.*

This Canaanite woman did not stop pleading with Jesus until He fulfilled her request. Jesus then told her that she was a woman of great faith.

Note the important connection between faith and persistence. Only a man or woman of faith will continue to press into God; they know God will answer in due time if they do not grow weary (Galatians 6:9).

What would have happened if this Canaanite woman gave up before Jesus responded? I believe her daughter would not have received her deliverance.

Another great example is found in Mark 10:46–52.

> *Then they came to Jericho. And as He was leaving Jericho with His disciples and a large crowd, a blind beggar named Bartimaeus, the son of Timaeus, was sitting by the road. When he heard that it was Jesus the Nazarene, he began to cry out and say, "Jesus Son of David, have mercy on me!" Many were sternly telling him to be quiet, but he kept crying out all the more, "Son of David, have mercy on me!" And Jesus stopped and said, "Call him here." So they called the blind man, saying to him, "Take courage, stand up! He is calling for you." Throwing aside his cloak, he jumped up and came to Jesus. And answering him, Jesus said, "What do you want Me to do for you?" And the blind man said to Him, "Rabboni, I want to regain my sight!" And Jesus said to him, "Go; your faith has made you well." Immediately he regained his sight and began following Him on the road.*

What would have happened if this blind man, Bartimaeus, listened to those who were telling him to be quiet? In all probability, he would not have been healed.

Jesus told Bartimaeus that his faith had made him well. In effect, his persistence in calling out to Jesus was an act of faith. Bartimaeus realized that Jesus was someone who could really help him, so he did not give up until Jesus touched him.

In Deuteronomy 9 we are told that God was going to destroy Israel for building the golden calf. Upon hearing this, Moses interceded on behalf of Israel for 40 days and nights until he knew that the Lord had answered him. What would have happened if Moses gave up after praying for only 32 days?

In 2 Kings 4, a Shunamite woman persisted in her pleading that Elisha would come and pray for her dead son. Elisha eventually went, and the boy was raised from the dead. Would that boy have been raised from the dead if his mother did not continue to press Elisha?

George Mueller said, "Never give up praying. I have been praying 63 years and eight months for one man's conversion. He is not saved yet, but he will be. How can it be otherwise? I am praying!" At Mueller's graveside service, this man finally did receive Christ. As Mueller's casket was being lowered into the grave, he fell on his knees and asked Jesus into his life.

PRAYER — THE FIRST STEP IN BATTLE

Persisting in prayer is very important because many times a spiritual battle must first be won before we can receive the answer to our petition.

The Apostle Paul clearly recognized that there was often a spiritual conflict that had to be won before prayers are answered.

Starting in Romans 15:30, Paul asked the Romans to strive in prayer for him because his opposition was great. He asked them to pray that he would be delivered from those who would want to stop the proclamation of the Gospel.

In Colossians 2:1–2, Paul tells the Colossians that he was struggling for them in prayer. In chapter four, Paul informs the Colossians that Epaphras was laboring earnestly for them in prayer.

Paul uses the words "struggling," "laboring," and "striving" to describe the type of prayer that was being prayed in these verses.

What were they striving, laboring and struggling against?

The *"rulers," "world forces of this darkness," "spiritual forces of wickedness,"* and the *"schemes of the devil"* (Ephesians 6:11–12).

Satan and all the hosts of hell fear persevering prayer and they will try anything to discourage us so we will quit praying. Satan may have the ability to hold back an answer or delay it for a while (Daniel 10), but he cannot delay it indefinitely!

Steady, persistent prayer:

- * Releases God's power
- * Breaks Satan's stronghold over a situation
- * Solidifies our commitment to keep praying until the answer comes.

Be assured; the answer will come.

Many of you reading this book are praying for things that as yet remain unanswered: finances, family turmoil, salvations, work situations, deep desires, etc.

Keep seeking, knocking, and asking!

Persistent prayer will bring an answer from God.

Remember, God always answers persistent prayer; He said he would, therefore He will.

There are far too many Christians who give up before seeing victory or experiencing an answer to their prayers. As I mentioned earlier Christians who tire of prayer often say something like, "It must be the will of God." Then they get really religious and justify their failure to keep praying as "submission to God's will."

This sounds very sanctimonious, but their failure to keep praying is nothing more than spiritual laziness. As a result they miss out on the victory God had planned for them. I do not want to miss out on any blessing the Lord has for me. Do you? I do not want my failure to pray or intercede to cause a slowing of God moving on the earth. Do you?

Of course not.

Make this commitment with me right now:

"I will never, Never, NEVER, **NEVER** give up in prayer until the answer comes."

CHAPTER FIVE

Prayer as Spiritual Warfare

In Ephesians 6:10–18, Paul tells us to stand firm and put on the "full armor of God" so we will be able to withstand the enemy's subtle, sudden attacks, schemes and deceptions. From this passage we come to understand that Paul is giving us a description of an enemy with whom we are in constant conflict.

These spiritual forces of wickedness are powerful, wicked haters of truth, shrewd, and ingeniously deceptive. They try to sway and deceive the world and negate the body of Christ. Their strategy is to influence our lifestyles, perceptions, values, attitudes, and anything else to neutralize us as effective soldiers in the Body of Christ.

Paul uses the analogy of a soldier in describing the weapons we use to confront these spiritual forces of wickedness. He selects six pieces of a Roman soldier's equipment to describe six different spiritual weapons we have as Christians. In verse 18, Paul gives us what I believe is our seventh spiritual weapon—prayer.

Have you ever wondered why the enemy puts such a high priority on undermining our prayer life?

He realizes we are in a spiritual battle, and he does not want us to enter this battle. He is afraid of Christians who get on their knees and release God's power against his schemes and strongholds.

Make no mistake, prayer is the one weapon that Satan fears most. Remember that the Bible tells us, *"The effective prayer of a righteous man can accomplish much"* (James 5:16).

I am convinced that the greatest battles we face in this life are first won or lost on our knees in prayer.

Satan does not want you to pray.

He will do anything to keep you off your knees.

He will lie and tell you, "Your prayers do not make a difference," or "Little happens when you pray." These are lies, and they come from the father of all lies.

Satan is not overly concerned with you and I unless we bathe all of our efforts for Christ in prayer.

PRAYER CONTROLS OUTCOMES

The major key to the success that our church has experienced in evangelism, children's ministry, youth ministry, and all our outreaches is due largely to prayer.

Our Prayer Society members have covenanted to pray a minimum of two and one half hours a week, not only for their own lives but for the church's staff and ministries.

Prayer has released God's power.

Prayer has broken Satan's strongholds in people's lives so that they can really see and hear God's direction.

Prayer is our greatest spiritual weapon, and we must first fight ALL of our battles, conflicts, and trials on our knees if we want to experience victory over them.

In Exodus 17 we find the Israelites defending themselves against the Amalekites because Israel had...

> *...journeyed by stages from the wilderness of Sin, according to the command of the Lord.*

The Israelites were stretched out for miles as they traveled. The sick and the elderly had to travel slowly, causing the column to stretch even further in the wilderness.

The Amalekites saw this as a great opportunity to plunder the Israelites. They figured they could attack quickly with their camels and be gone before the Israelites could muster a defense (Deuteronomy 25:17-19). It was no secret that the Israelites had left Egypt loaded down with wealth (Exodus 12:31-36), and the Amalekites viewed the Israelites as easy prey.

In Exodus 17, Moses commanded Joshua to choose men to go and attack the Amalekites before they could do anymore damage. As the battle began, Moses, Aaron, and Hur climbed atop a mountain where Moses stood with his staff, a symbol of God's presence. As the two armies fought, Moses raised his staff and Israel prevailed. But, when his arms grew tired and he lowered his staff, the Amalekites prevailed. It soon became apparent to Moses, Aaron, and Hur that the determining factor in the battle was whether or not Moses held up his staff. Immediately upon discerning this, Aaron and Hur sat Moses down on a rock and held up his arms until the sun set. We are told in Exodus 17, "*Joshua overwhelmed Amalek and his people with the edge of the sword.*"

This story is significant because the battle was not won due to any superiority in Israel's military skill or equipment. The battle was won on top of that mountain

There is a very important biblical principle concerning prayer that we can glean from this story. God wants us to understand that there was much more going on than two armies fighting. God's message here is that in every situation or conflict in our church, city, or in our own lives, the outcome is not necessarily controlled by what we see or experience but rather by what happens in our place of prayer.

SUPERNATURAL VICTORIES OVER SATAN

Over and over again in the Old Testament God brought His people to a place where they were totally outnumbered and outgunned, facing overwhelming odds.

Nevertheless, they would experience a supernatural victory.

Why?

Because someone looked to God in total dependence. They came to understand that the deciding factor in these situations was not always what they perceived in the physical realm but what was determined in the spiritual.

This story of Israel shows us that we must look to God in prayer concerning each and every battle we face. So often in the battles of our lives, the church, and in our cities and nation, we do not know who the real enemy is. We think it is our boss, the neighbor, the city, a relative, a co-worker, a city council member or a teacher.

No.

The Bible tells us our real enemy is Satan.

If we do not first fight our battles in prayer, we will make the wrong people our enemies. They may appear to be our foes, but the real enemy is the satanic power behind them.

It is my firm belief that if we want our loved ones to be saved and our cities and nation to change, then we must pray against the powers that are influencing them.

First, we must pray against the demonic spirits, strongholds, and deceptions that keep our loved ones from understanding the truth.

Secondly, we must pray against the principalities of evil that influence our cities and nation. In Mark 3:27, Jesus explains it this way:

> *But no one can enter the strong man's house and plunder his property unless he first binds the strong man, and then he will plunder his house.*

Jesus is saying that before we can plunder the enemy's kingdom, we must first bind demonic strongholds. We must develop the habit of binding the enemy's control over people, places, and events as we pray for spiritual breakthroughs. If we are going to do this—pray against principalities, powers, world forces of darkness, and demonic strongholds—then we need to understand two important truths about prayer and spiritual warfare.

The first truth is that our Lord has given us power and authority over the demonic and evil strongholds in this world. Paul prays in Ephesians 1 that the hearts of the Ephesians would be enlightened to their inheritance and...

> *...what is the surpassing greatness of his power toward us who believe.*

He reminds the Ephesians that the resurrected Christ is...

...far above all rule and authority and power and dominion... He put all things in subjection under His feet.

Paul's prayer is that you and I would really understand how Christ's death and resurrection dealt Satan and his kingdom a death blow. Jesus' victory at Calvary and His resurrection three days later have literally put all of Satan's power in subjection under the feet of Jesus.

We regularly need to remind ourselves that Jesus came to earth to destroy forever the works of the devil (1 John 3:8, Colossians 2:15). In Ephesians 2:4-6, we read:

But God, being rich in mercy, because of His great love with which He loved us, even when we were dead in our transgressions, made us alive together with Christ (by grace you have been saved), and raised us up with Him, and seated us with Him in the heavenly places in Christ Jesus.

Paul tells us that we are seated with Christ in heavenly places. We are Christ's ambassadors, and as we serve Him we carry His authority against any demonic power that would stand in our way. We have a responsibility to bind and hinder all that needs to be overcome in order to see God's Kingdom come in our world.

Please understand that Jesus' death and resurrection defeated Satan, and God has placed the enforcement of Calvary's victory in the hands of His church.

Jesus has given us the power of attorney. We are Jesus' ambassadors, His deputies. We have His delegated authority to literally speak for Christ.

When I think of the implications of this, it reminds me of our great responsibility to bring about God's Kingdom here on the earth.

Friend, you and I have been called to push back the demonic in our world. We cannot pretend the demonic does not exist, or be afraid, or live our lives hoping someone else will do our work for us.

God has called us to battle.

We are to engage the enemy whenever or wherever he hinders the advancement of God's Kingdom.

What does this mean in practical terms?

BIND THE STRONGHOLDS IN YOUR LIFE

It means you and I are to bind and pray against demonic strongholds and influences in our own lives, and in the lives of those around us. For example, you may be married to a man who simply has no interest in the Gospel. He may think it is all right for you, but he tells you, "Don't push your religion on me." This husband has a dullness over his life that must be broken before he will understand his need for a savior.

Your son or daughter may be using drugs and living a wild life. What is needed is prayer against that demonic lie concerning friends, the world's values, perverted pleasures and so forth.

You may be coming out of a life of bondage to drugs or alcohol. You need to pray against the demonic lies and evil spiritual influences that have controlled your life for so long.

The list could be endless.

With each new situation, God will give you the wisdom on how to pray against the demonic strongholds, bondages and lies that have hindered God's influence on individuals, situations, or even your own life.

As we use our authority against the demonic in prayer, there is a second truth we must understand: there is a proper way to address or speak to the demonic.

Demonic spirits have authority and power given to them by God.

The gifts and the calling of God are irrevocable.
(Romans 11: 29)

These evil spirits rebelled against God and now use this authority and power for the kingdom of darkness. In the book of Jude, verse 9, we read:

> *But Michael the archangel, when he disputed with the devil and argued about the body of Moses, did not dare pronounce against him a railing judgment, but said, "The Lord rebuke you!"*

I have never read a commentary that could explain to my satisfaction what was going on in this passage. It is one of those scriptures that will remain a mystery until heaven.

But, I do believe we can draw one sure conclusion from this passage: Michael the archangel was careful how he addressed Satan.

Why?

Because Satan does have power, a lot of power, originally given to him by God.

Notice how Michael uses God's authority—not his own—when speaking directly to the devil. I am convinced this is a very important lesson for all Christians when praying against the demonic. We must remember that we are ambassadors; we are messengers. We are not the King. Our only power comes through the name of Jesus, and the fact that the Holy Spirit has made His abode with us.

BE WARNED

If you pray against the demonic while practicing sin or pray very flippantly, pridefully, or arrogantly, you leave yourself vulnerable to attack from the enemy.

Whenever I pray against the kingdom of darkness, I literally tell the spirit or spirits that I am only carrying out the orders of my Lord Jesus. I am coming against them merely as the Lord's representative, and that Jesus has given me authority over them as a result of Calvary and Easter morning. Therefore, I command them to leave, be pushed back, remove their hold, release the confusion, or that their deception would be exposed.

> *In short, I speak as an ambassador of Christ. The evil spirits must respond because God "is above all.*
>
> (Ephesians 4:6 KJV).

When I rebuke a spiritual stronghold or an evil spirit, I want that spirit to see Jesus standing next to me. I want them to see the host of Heaven over my right shoulder. I want them to shake with fear knowing that Jesus is saying in effect, "Do not mess with My child. He speaks for Me. Mess with him and you mess with Me!"

BEWARE OF PRIDE

My friend, never command or rebuke evil spirits in your own pride or arrogance or you may pay a price; these beings do have power. But, if you command or rebuke them in godly humility, understanding who you are and in total dependence on God, you thwart any effort on their part to torment you.

In James 4:7 (NKJV), he tells us to *"submit to God."* Later, he says,

Resist the devil and he will flee from you.

There is a logical progression here. When we understand our total dependence on God and know that we cannot possibly do anything alone, then we are able to successfully resist the devil.

Be assured that I am not saying we shouldn't be bold. Who wouldn't be fearless with Jesus standing next to them? Imagine: we have the whole host of Heaven right behind us!

You and I never have to fear the demonic. It is they who have to fear us. Do not be a sideline Christian; enter the battle.

> *The weapons of our warfare are... divinely powerful for the destruction of fortresses.*
>
> (2 Corinthians 10:4)

Your greatest weapon against the kingdom of darkness is prayer.

CHAPTER SIX

Prayer and Obedience

I do not think it is possible to write a book on prayer and not mention a few things about the foundational relationship between prayer and obedience.

Everywhere in Scripture God is represented as rewarding obedience and punishing disobedience.

If you read Deuteronomy 27-30, it becomes obvious that our experience in this life is determined to a great extent by our obedience or disobedience to God. The Bible also tells us that God never changes and that sin (disobedience) separates us from God (Isaiah 59:2).

If we want to pray effectively and hear God speak to us, we must be committed to obedience.

The type of obedience God is looking for is the humble decision to surrender our will to Him and submit ourselves to the commands of His Holy Scriptures.

For us as Christians, there is only one reason we disobey: rebellion, a conscious decision to disobey God. Rebellion is usually clothed with every conceivable excuse, rationalization, and compromise.

Jesus had a very penetrating question for all of us to ponder in Luke 6:46.

> *Why do you call me "Lord, Lord," and not do what I say?*

In James 5:16-18 God tells us that:

> *The effective prayer of a righteous man can accomplish much. Elijah was a man with a nature like ours, and he prayed earnestly that it would not rain, and it did not rain on the earth for three years and six months. Then he prayed again, and the sky poured rain and the earth produced its fruit.*

When you read this passage, don't you want to know what an effective prayer is and how to pray that kind of prayer? To me, an effective prayer is one that gets results, just like Elijah prayed so long ago. Please note, this passage tells us that Elijah was a man, a human being, with frailties just like us. Therefore, isn't James telling us we can pray just as effectively as Elijah?

The answer to this question is a resounding yes.

According to this passage, it is the righteous man who is able to pray the effective prayer. How does the Bible define who is a righteous man? In Habakkuk 2:4 we are told that the *"righteous live by... faith."* Habakkuk is describing a man or woman who believes God's Word and obeys it. That is real faith.

OBEDIENCE IS FAITH IN ACTION

Real faith shows itself in obedience to the Word of God. The Apostle James states this same idea when he writes, *"Faith without works is dead"* (James 2:26).

What is a work?

An act of obedience.

We can therefore conclude that faith without obedience is dead.

It seems apparent to me that a commitment to obedience brings about effective praying—prayer that gets results. A righteous man is an obedient man, and it is he who can pray effectively.

> *For the eyes of the Lord are toward the righteous, and*
> *His ears attend to their prayer.*
>
> (1 Peter 3:12)
>
> *But to this one I will look, to him who is humble and*
> *contrite of spirit, and who trembles at My word.*
>
> (Isaiah 66:2)
>
> *The righteous cry, and the Lord hears and delivers them*
> *out of all their troubles.*
>
> (Psalm 34:17)

In 2 Kings 20, we are told that King Hezekiah "*became mortally ill*" and that Isaiah the prophet visited him and said,

> *Thus says the Lord, "Set your house in order for you*
> *shall die and not live."*

After hearing this, King Hezekiah prayed and reminded the Lord how he had…

> *…walked before You in truth and with a whole heart and*
> *have done what is good in Your sight.*

Before we go any further, let us look back and learn a little bit about King Hezekiah. He was twenty-five years old when he became king, and he did…

...right in the sight of the Lord... He removed the high places... cut down the Asherah [idol worship]. He trusted in the Lord, the God of Israel; so that after him there was none like him among all the kings of Judah... For he clung to the Lord... kept His commandments... and the Lord was with him.

(2 Kings 18:1-7)

This passage shows that Hezekiah was obedient to the Lord's command. He was not only obedient, but he was aggressive in his desire to please the Lord.

In 2 Kings 20 we are further told that Isaiah the prophet had not *"gone out of the middle court"* before the Lord spoke to Isaiah and told him that He had heard King Hezekiah's prayer, and that in three days he would be healed.

Did King Hezekiah's prayer get results?

You bet it did.

The prophet Isaiah hadn't even left the palace before God answered the prayer. King Hezekiah cried out to God to remember his obedience and his desire to please Him in all areas of his life.

Friend, the Lord hears the prayers of the righteous (the obedient), and He *"attend[s] to their prayer"* (1 Peter 3:12). E. M. Bounds said, "An obedient life helps prayer... it speeds the prayer to the throne of God."

Obedience is the basis for effective prayer.

Obedience ultimately brings us close to God.

When we pursue obedience, it usually requires that we exercise faith. We know from scripture that faith pleases God (Hebrews 11:6).

The writer of Hebrews also tells us that we will not be able to see (understand) God without our sanctification (Hebrews 12:14).

What is our sanctification?

The process by which we are transformed into the image of Christ.

How does this happen?

Through a conscious, daily decision to be obedient. That decision results in a transformation of our lives. Then, as our minds are renewed (sanctified), we are able to understand the will of God (Romans 12:2).

DISOBEDIENCE DESTROYS INTIMACY

In John 14, Jesus gives us a very important truth concerning the relationship between obedience and our closeness to God.

> *"If you love Me, you will keep My commandments... He who has My commandments and keeps them is the one who loves me; and he who loves Me will be loved by My Father, and I will love him and will disclose Myself to him"...Jesus answered and said to him, "If anyone loves Me, he will keep My word; and My Father will love him, and We will come to him and make Our abode with him."*

> (John 14:15, 21, 23)

These verses clearly state that our intimacy or closeness to God is related to our obedience. Our ability to be heard and to hear from God is also associated with our obedience.

This illustration is not perfect, but it does help to illustrate an important point. Consider this: You have two teenage sons, both in high school. One son is constantly disobeying you; it seems as if he does just the opposite of what you ask of him. Your other son has some moments of rebellion (always with repentance), but almost always respects and obeys you. You dearly love both sons but which son would you be the most proud of? Which son would you have the most affection for? Which son would most readily receive the requests he made of you? Which would you trust with important responsibilities in the family?

Obviously, the answer to all these questions is the obedient son; he has shown his love and trustworthiness by obedience.

Do not ever be fooled into thinking that you can simply rely on God's love, mercy, and forgiveness to overlook disobedience. God cannot overlook sin. There are always consequences for rebellious disobedience. One consequence is that your prayer life will be affected.

Disobedience (sin) always puts a separation between you and God (Isaiah 59:2). Before God can work further in your life, sin must be addressed.

Have you ever had a close friend say or do something that hurt you deeply? If you have, you understand how that relationship was affected. That friendship cannot continue to grow until the issue is addressed. While this is not a perfect example of our relationship with God, it does give an understanding of how sin can cause a barrier between us and our Lord.

If obedience to God isn't a priority in our lives, our prayers are going to be weak and religious; we will see little results.

Why is this?

Because our obedience is related to our intimacy with God.

Our Lord surely hears all of our prayers, but He is stopped from answering or acting on our requests because of disobedience. I am sure that there have been times when you have gone to the Lord in prayer only to find that the Lord gently and lovingly reminded you of a sin that needed to be eliminated.

Then, as you confessed and repented from that sin, you felt the barrier lifted between you and God.

We must remember we serve a holy God who cannot tolerate sin. He sent His son Jesus to die in our place for our sins so that we might have a relationship with God and inherit eternal life. If sin is so serious that the Father sent His own Son to die for our sins, can we honestly imagine that God would overlook sin in our lives?

OBEDIENCE BRINGS BLESSINGS

The Lord is waiting for many of us to learn obedience so He can bless us with every spiritual blessing. God wants to give us direction, wisdom, success, and be intimate with us, but He is restrained because of persistent disobedience.

In Deuteronomy 1 and 2, Moses recounts how Israel decided to attack the Amorites even though God specifically told them not to. They rebelled, thinking they knew best, going their own way.

The result was that...

> *The Amorites who lived in that hill country came out against you and chased you as bees do, and crushed you from Seir to Hormah.*

When the Israelites returned from this defeat, they...

> *...wept before the Lord; but the Lord did not listen to your voice nor give ear to you.*

Why wouldn't the Lord listen to the Israelites?

Because of their disobedience.

Soon after this episode, God directed Moses to take the Israelites back into the wilderness and circle Mt. Seir "*for many days.*" After those many days had passed, God told Moses,

> *You have circled the mountain long enough. Now turn north.*

Can you see what was happening?

God couldn't give the Israelites any more directions until they learned obedience. They had to wait a little longer before going into the Promised Land. The Lord had to make sure they learned obedience because He had specific plans that He wanted them to implement to the letter.

Once the Lord knew they had learned obedience—but not before—He gave them direction.

Many Christians earnestly desire answers to their prayers, are fixed on God's promises, and persist in prayer, yet nothing ever seems to happen. It is my experience that a good part of what people call "unanswered prayer" is really a result of sin, compromise, and disobedience in their lives.

In Revelation 3:16, Jesus tells the Laodicean church that because they were…

> *…neither hot or cold, I will spit you out of my mouth.*

What is a lukewarm Christian?

A person who has little passion for Christ and His commands and compromises holy living through disobedience.

Jesus further tells John in Revelation 3:17, because of its lukewarmness the church was *"wretched and miserable and poor and blind and naked."* The church was spiritually dull, lifeless, without vision, lacking power, and walking outside of God's promises. When we walk outside of God's promises, we walk in disobedience and sin, separating us from God.

Ultimately, sin and disobedience affect our prayer life.

The scriptures are clear concerning the relationship between prayer and obedience, and we must remember that God does not change (Psalm 15:4).

If you want to have an effective prayer life, you m̲ ̲ ̲ ̲r heart on obeying God and readily acknowledge, confes̲ ̲ ̲ ̲ ̲n sin in your life.

CHAPTER SEVEN

Hearing the Voice of God in Prayer

One cry common among Christians is, "We want to know the will of God, to hear God speak to us. We want to be sure it is God that we are hearing. We do not want to be confused or deceived. We simply want to hear the voice of God."

It has been my experience that God speaks to us in six ways:

1. Through His Word
2. Through the counsel of other Christians
3. Through a still small voice during the day
4. Through dreams or visions
5. During our times of prayer
6. Circumstances.

In this chapter I will concentrate on the importance of hearing the voice of God during our devotional and prayer times.

Jesus' death and resurrection defeated sin, death, and the devil for all time. It also broke a barrier that existed between mankind and God because of sin.

The relationship that God enjoyed with Adam and Eve before the Fall is now reestablished to a great degree. Obviously, we do not have the same perfect relationship because we still struggle with sin, and Adam and Eve were created without sin.

Nevertheless, the barrier that separated mankind from God has been dealt with, and our ability to hear and interact with God has been reestablished. You and I can now have an intimate, personal relationship with the Lord God Almighty.

We can talk to Him and hear Him speak to us.

Isn't a relationship always a two-way exchange?

Unfortunately, too often our relationship with God is simply a one-way conversation, nothing more than a litany of requests. While these requests may be appropriate, genuine prayer includes listening and hearing God's voice.

Imagine a relationship with someone who did all the talking. Try as you would, you could never initiate a conversation or respond to anything the other person said.

Would this really be a relationship?

Of course not!

A relationship, by definition, is a two-way exchange.

A Personal Relationship... With God?

In John 17:3, Jesus prays for His disciples and says:

This is eternal life, that they may know You, the only true God, and Jesus Christ whom You have sent.

Our eternal life, our salvation is not simply a possession or right. It is also a relationship. The Greek word "to know" (*ginosko*) that is used in this passage does not simply refer to a casual relationship. In the Septuagint, the Greek translation of the Old Testament, "ginosko" is used to translate the Hebrew word *yada,* which has a basic meaning of "experiencing something" and "to know by learning."

This experience becomes reality in a relationship based on familiarity with the person or thing known. To know another person face-to-face means to have a personal and confidential relationship with him[2] (Deuteronomy 34:10).

It is quite clear to me that in John's writings he uses the word "ginosko" to describe an inner fellowship between Jesus and His people. For example:

> *I am the good shepherd; and I know My own and My own know me.*

(John 10:14)

> *But you know Him because He abides with you and will be in you.*

(John 14:17)

The Greek word "ginosko" can also mean, "to have sexual relations with." It is translated in just this way in the Septuagint (Genesis 4:1) where Adam *knew* Eve. "Ginosko" can then refer to the intimacy between a husband and a wife.

Part of our eternal life, part of our experience as Christians is to know God in an intimate and personal way. This is why people often say, "Christianity is not a religion but a relationship."

In Isaiah 62:5 we are told,

---

[2]   Dictionary of New Testament Theology, Volume 2, Editor Colin Brown.

*As the bridegroom rejoices over the bride, so your God
will rejoice over you.*

Think about this.

God loves you as a bridegroom loves his bride.

In the fourth chapter of the Song of Solomon, King Solomon is
addressing his bride, telling her how he loves her and is anticipating
being with her. In verse nine and ten he tells his bride:

> *You have made my heart beat faster, my sister, my bride;
> You have made my heart beat faster with a single glance
> of your eyes... How beautiful is your love, my sister, my
> bride!*

These verses describe a man who is passionately in love with his
bride. It is hard to imagine, but the Bible tells us that this is how our
Lord Jesus loves us! He longs to be with us; He literally gets excited
when we take the time to be alone with Him, to speak to Him.

I do not know about you, but I have a trouble with all this. It is hard
for me to picture God Almighty loving me with this kind of emotion and
intensity, that His heart beats faster when I take time to be alone with
Him. Nevertheless, He does, because that is how the Bible describes
His love for us.

Most of us probably have trouble with this type of description of
God's love because too few of us have taken the time to experience
God's presence, listen for His voice, or simply be alone with Him.

It seems clear to me from Scripture that our Lord not only loves
us but also desires to have a relationship with us. Genuine prayer is a
two-way exchange involving not only us speaking to the Lord but also
listening for Him to speak back.

GOD SPEAKS TO HIS PEOPLE

In Habakkuk 2:1–2 we read about the prophet Habakkuk going to his place of prayer to be alone with God so that he can hear His voice.

> *I will stand on my guard post and station myself on the rampart; And I will keep watch to see what He will speak to me, and how I may reply when I am reproved. Then the Lord answered me and said...*

Notice that Habakkuk went to be alone with God, and that he expected the Lord to speak to him.

The Gospel writers often mention the fact that Jesus would often slip away alone to pray. In Mark 1:35, Mark tells us that Jesus arose early and...

> *...went away to a secluded place, and was praying there.*

His disciples, after awakening, began to look for Him. When they found Him they said, "Everyone is looking for you." He responded by saying that they must leave and go to the towns nearby so they could preach there also. Obviously, the Lord had spoken to Him and given Him directions about where He was to go next.

In Luke 6:12, Jesus went to a mountain to pray. When He returned, He selected His twelve disciples.

In Luke 9, Jesus' disciples came to Him "*while He was praying.*" Before they could say anything, He asked them a question that prompted the teaching that to save one's life, one must first lose it.

Jesus' actions after a time of prayer should remind us that Jesus said only what the Father told Him to speak (John 14:10). Therefore, we can conclude that one of the reasons Jesus spent time alone with God in prayer was so He could hear God speak to Him.

Now, we do not necessarily have to be alone to hear God's voice. But, if we do not practice hearing God in the stillness and quiet of our devotional time, how will we ever hear His voice in the midst of a noisy, busy day?

All through Scripture we have hundreds of examples of the Lord speaking to His people.

Genesis 12:1
Now the Lord said to Abram...

Exodus 4:4
The Lord said to Moses...

Exodus 7:8
Now the Lord spoke to Moses and Aaron...

Joshua 4:1
The Lord spoke to Joshua...

1 Samuel 3:11
The Lord said to Samuel...

Isaiah 8:1
Then the Lord said to me...

Ezekiel 1:3
The word of the Lord came expressly to Ezekiel...

John 5:30
As I hear I judge...

Acts 8:29
Then the Spirit said to Philip...

Acts 11:12
The Spirit told me...

Hebrews 12:25

See to it that you do not refuse Him who is speaking...

Revelation 1:10–11

And I heard behind me a loud voice like the sound of a trumpet saying...

After reading all of these scriptures, are we to believe God has stopped speaking to His people? Is there a passage in the New Testament that tells us we can no longer hear His voice?

Remember, the Lord does not change (Psalm 55:19). "*Jesus Christ is the same yesterday and today and forever.*" (Hebrews 13:8)

God still desires to speak to His people.

Let's look at a few of the scriptures that exhort us to listen for the voice of God:

If you will listen to the voice of the Lord your God...
(Deuteronomy 13:18)

Whether it is pleasant or unpleasant, we will listen to the voice of the Lord.
(Jeremiah 42:6)

Heed instruction and be wise, and do not neglect it. Blessed is the man who listens to me, watching daily at my gates, waiting at my doorposts.
(Proverbs 8:33–34)

I will hear what God the Lord will say.
(Psalm 85:8)

Come, let us worship and bow down, let us kneel before the Lord our Maker. For He is our God, and we are the

people of His pasture and the sheep of His hand. Today,
if you hear His voice, do not harden your hearts.

(Psalms 95:6-8)

Give ear and hear my voice, listen and hear my words.

(Isaiah 28:23)

Listen carefully to Me... incline your ear and come to
Me. Listen, that you may live.

(Isaiah 55:2-3)

The sheep hear his voice... the sheep follow him because
they know his voice... My sheep hear My voice, and I
know them.

(John 10: 3, 4, 27)

It is clear from these passages, and especially from the words of Jesus, that God expects His people to hear His voice.

In the Old Testament we are told that the Lord spoke to Elijah (1 Kings 17:2), and James tells us that Elijah had a nature just like ours (James 5:17).

GENUINE PRAYER IS AN EXCHANGE

The real issue is whether you and I will take time to be alone with God in prayer, learning to hear His voice. Genuine prayer is not merely asking for things; it involves a relationship, a two-way exchange.

In 1 Corinthians 2:7-16, Paul tells us quite plainly that we are taught the things of God through the Holy Spirit that lives inside of us. We literally have a divine receiver inside of us that can hear the voice of God. Paul tells us that God's Holy Spirit is given so "*that we may know the things freely given to us by God*" (verse 12).

We hear the voice of God in our spirit! We need to spend time with God and learn to hear His voice speaking to us.

Before going any further, let's look at a few verses from the Book of

John:

> *But I tell you the truth, it is to your advantage that I go away; for if I do not go away, the Helper will not come to you; but if I go, I will send Him to you... But when He, the Spirit of truth, comes, He will guide you into all the truth; for He will not speak on His own initiative, but whatever He hears, He will speak.*
>
> (John 16:7, 13)

> *I will ask the Father, and He will give you another Helper, that He may be with you forever; that is the Spirit of truth, whom the world cannot receive, because it does not see Him or know Him, but you know Him because He abides with you and will be in you.*
>
> (John 14:16-17)

God has made His abode with you and wants to speak to you. One of the responsibilities of the Holy Spirit is to speak to you, to speak God's heart, to give you direction and reveal spiritual truths about the Kingdom of God.

My friend, Jesus our Lord loves you and wants to be intimate with you. He wants you to know His voice. The only obstacle that we face in our pursuit of this relationship is our own unwillingness to spend time alone with God in prayer.

Hopefully, in the remainder of this chapter, I will accomplish two things:

1. I will give you a concrete method to begin to practice hearing the voice of God.

2. When you think you have heard a word from the Lord, you will know how to test it to make sure it was from God.

HOW TO HEAR GOD'S VOICE

The Apostle John told us to test the spirits (1 John 4:1) to make sure we are hearing from God. Frankly, I have found it fairly easy to discern the voice of God by using an eight-fold test I will explain to you a little later in this chapter.

Before we go any further, some of you might find all this talk about listening for God's voice a bit unsettling. You probably have this mental picture of someone sitting down and listening for a voice, which often does lead to deception. Many of the false New Age and eastern philosophies seek spirit guides in somewhat similar ways. These people do have spiritual encounters, but they are contacting and communicating with demonic spirits. We as Christians have communion with the Holy Spirit.

The presence of a counterfeit is proof that there is a real item! No one would counterfeit a $25 bill... they'd counterfeit a $20 bill.

Dear Christian, I implore you, do not be afraid of listening for the voice of God, even though there are deceptions in the world. If you are careful and follow the safeguards I will share in this chapter, you will not be deceived; it is impossible.

Now, let us look at a good five-fold method to begin practicing to hear the voice of God during our prayer time.

• WE MUST BE EXPECTANT

When we are alone with God in prayer, we must believe He will speak to us. We must take Him at His Word and trust that He is the rewarder of those that seek Him (Hebrews 11:6). We should say as the young Samuel did so long ago, "*Speak, for Your servant is listening*" (1 Samuel 3:4-10). When His Word says,

> *Call to Me and I will answer you, and I will tell you great and mighty things, which you do not know.*
>
> (Jeremiah 33:3)

He means it.

God does not lie.

If He tells you that He is going to speak awesome things to you, that is exactly what He is going to do!

• WE MUST BE COMMITTED TO OBEY

Be willing to hear that which we may not really want to hear. For example, God may say, "Son, I want you to be reconciled with your brother," or "Ask that sister to forgive you," or "Go witness to that co-worker," or "Give Mr. and Mrs. Jones $500.00," or "I want you to teach in the Children's Church." If we really want the Lord to speak to us, we must be willing to obey Him even before we know what our Lord would have us do.

• MAKE TIME TO BE ALONE WITH GOD

I'm absolutely convinced that you and I will not hear the voice of God if we do not first practice hearing His voice in our quiet place of prayer. Each of us needs to regularly go to a private and safe place to be alone with God, to pray and listen for His voice.

- **DURING PRAYER BE QUIET AND LISTEN FOR HIS VOICE**

Ask the Lord if there is something He would like to say to you each day. If you are burdened by a situation, and prayed for wisdom, listen to hear God's insight. Often during the last 20 years, God has given me insight into people's problems and circumstances as I waited on Him and listened for His voice.

- **DO NOT GET FRUSTRATED**

My friend, God will speak to you if you persist in listening for His Voice. Do not think that the first time you get alone and listen for two minutes that you'll hear God speak to you. It is possible but not probable.

In the book of Hebrews, Chapter 5, we are told that we need to train our senses. We must train our spirits to recognize and distinguish the voice of God. But I guarantee if you begin listening for God during your quiet time, He will speak to you.

I cannot tell you how many times God has given me wisdom, ideas or direction while I was in prayer. Once about ten years ago I was praying, asking God how we could stimulate prayer in the church. We'd tried for years to encourage our people to come to our corporate prayer meetings, but our attendance had always been small in comparison with Sunday mornings. While in prayer, God gave me the idea for our Prayer Society, which has increased prayer in our church a hundredfold (see my chapter on the Prayer Society). The Prayer Society has worked so well because it wasn't my idea—it was God's!

The most radical way God has spoken to me was during prayer while I was in seminary in 1983. I was facing one of the most difficult decisions of my life: whether or not to leave the denomination of my birth. The long-term ramifications of this decision would affect me financially and with friends and family.

One morning I got alone with God in one of the small typing rooms in the library. I knelt down and began to pray, asking for wisdom. I needed to make a decision soon because they were beginning to hand out intern assignments. As I prayed, God's presence filled the room! I stood up, raised my hands and began praising God. After a few minutes, His presence left and I sat down. I looked over at the typewriter and there was a typed message for me. This astounded me, since I know for a fact that there wasn't any paper in that typewriter before I began to pray. The message from God read, "David, in the near future you shall meet a man with dark hair and double lenses. Keep this in mind as you move on to the greater things in life."

A few days later a man with dark hair and bifocals—a man I had never met—walked up to me and said, "Are you considering leaving the _____ denomination? Because if you are, I'd like to introduce you to a particular denomination I think you'd really like." He then proceeded to tell me about this denomination and encouraged me to give them a call.

I did contact his denomination and ministered there for several years before my brother and I were lead by God to start Foothills Christian Church.

Here's my point: when we need direction, wisdom, or discernment, God will go to great lengths to see that we receive what we ask for. Remember, I'm nothing special. There is no partiality with God (Romans 2:11). God loves you and wants to speak to you just as much as He wants to speak to me.

God wants to speak to His people if only we will give Him the opportunity.

HOW TO TEST WHAT YOU THINK YOU HEARD

Finally, let's answer the questions, "What do I do with a word that I think I have heard from God?" and, "How can I be sure it was really Him speaking, especially if what I believe God said to me involves risk, financial or otherwise?"

I'm sure you are familiar with the passage in 1 John that exhorts us to test what we hear in the spiritual realm to make sure it is from the Lord (1 John 4:1–6).

There is a surefire, eight-fold test you can use to guarantee that you will never be deceived. I have never seen anyone who tested what they heard by using this method miss God or fall into error.

1. Does the "word" agree with Scripture?

Ask this question first. God will NEVER contradict Himself since God never changes (Psalm 15:4). He is reliable and faithful. If you think God has spoken to you and the direction is in disagreement with His Word, it wasn't Him. If somehow you think God has given you a revelation that supersedes His Word—make no mistake, you are in deception!

As a pastor I have seen many Christians suffer greatly because they adamantly believed God had spoken to them that it was okay to trespass Scripture. As I write this chapter, a women in our church is convinced that God has spoken to her, telling her to marry a particular man she knows, a man who is not Christian.

Would God speak this to her?

Of course not (2 Corinthians 6:14).

God will never contradict His Word.

I'm sure you can understand how important it is to know the Word of God if you are interested in hearing God speak to you. We must have the discernment that God's word gives us to distinguish between God's voice and "other voices."

2. It should challenge your faith.

Will obedience to the Word you think God has given you cause you to step out, trust God, and mature in your walk with the Lord?

God is always concerned with our sanctification.

God is concerned with us growing up into maturity.

If you are challenged to take a step of faith or steps toward holiness, then there is a good chance God is speaking to you. The Bible says, *"Without faith it is impossible to please Him"* (Hebrews 11:6).

3. Does the "word" go against worldly wisdom?

For My thoughts are not your thoughts, nor are your ways My ways," declares the Lord. "For as the heavens are higher than the earth, so are My ways higher than your ways and My thoughts than your thoughts.

(Isaiah 55:8–9)

If you believe you have received a word, and it is something that seems illogical, going against worldly wisdom, it quite possibly could be from God. Often what He tells us to do goes against the good advice of the day. It is as if He is testing us in an effort to increase our faith and trust in Him and His promises.

But be warned!

I am not suggesting you throw all common sense out the window. This is only one of the signs or attributes of God's voice. If you base your decision on whether you are hearing God solely on this one test you will get into trouble. However, God often will tell us to do something that goes contrary to worldly wisdom.

4. Take the "word" to mature Christians.

Often I take what I believe I have heard from the Lord to other godly, mature men for their confirmation. This needs to be a mature Christian, someone to whom you have submitted your life (a Pastor, Home Group leader, Elder, Bible study leader, Counselor, etc.). These individuals should know the Word of God and speak the truth to you in love, sharing honestly what they really think.

Proverb 13:10 declares,

> *But wisdom is with those who receive counsel.*

Again, in Proverb 12:15, it says,

> *A wise man is he who listens to counsel.*

Finally, in Proverb 11:14 we read,

> *In abundance of counselors there is victory.*

This is a very important test in verifying the voice of God!

I would never make any decision in my life or the church without first submitting it to men to whom I have submitted my life. I see these men as a blessing in my life; they help me not to miss God, and to avoid deception. If God is really speaking to me, I know these mature Christians will recognize God's voice and confirm it.

5. Does the "word" cause you to take a stand for Christ?

If you follow this word, will it make you take a stand for Christ? Will your coworkers and other nonbelievers be apprised of your obedience to Christ? Does it cause a banner to be raised over your life that reads, Christian, follower of Jesus Christ?

The last thing Satan wants is for us to let other people know we are Christians, telling them that only Jesus has the way, truth and the life. Satan does not want anyone to stand up and be counted for Christ, bringing God's light into the world! If following through on a word that you think is from God causes you to take a stand for Christ in this "evil and perverse generation," it could very well be God.

6. Is the "word" wanting you to rush?

Nowhere in the Word of God are we told to rush into anything. Proverb 19:2 says, *"He who hurries his footsteps errs."*

If you believe you heard from God and He's telling you to forgo all restraints and rush into something, it probably is not God. Satan wants us to act impulsively; he does not want us to seek counsel or consider the ramifications or consequences of our behavior.

Satan wants you to go it alone, to be filled with pride, thinking somehow you have a special pipeline to God. The devil wants your faith to crumble, and he is hoping you will ultimately blame God for the consequences of a quick decision.

As a pastor I have seen many Christians make mistakes in their lives simply because they did not take the time to test what they thought God was telling them.

7. Peace

Initially, when we hear God speak to us, there may be great struggle, anxiety, fear, and conflict because of what we believe the Lord wants us to do. But as we pray, seek counsel and test what we have heard, if it is the Lord, the conflict will be replaced by the peace of God. We still might be apprehensive about what is to come, but God will give us His peace if we are hearing from Him.

In Philippians 4:6–7, Paul tells us,

> *Be anxious for nothing, but in everything by prayer and supplication with thanksgiving let your requests be made known to God. And the peace of God, which surpasses all comprehension, will guard your hearts and your minds in Christ Jesus.*

As we pray, seeking God's assurance and wisdom, He not only will give us discernment, but if He is speaking, will give us His peace.

8. Fruit

If the word you hear brings fear, bondage, anxiety, confusion, lust, and division, then the fruit is evil and the word is not from the Lord.

On the other hand, if you see that the word causes you to grow in faith and helps you to develop godly characteristics and pursue holiness, then it probably is from the Lord.

As I close this chapter, let me remind you that the Bible tells us to *"examine everything carefully"* (1 Thessalonians 5:21). If you believe you have heard the voice of God, test and examine that word to make sure it is from the Lord and not from your own heart, imagination, or from the enemy. This testing pleases our Lord because it demonstrates obedience and protects you from being deceived.

I don't know about you, but I want to hear the voice of God. Therefore I'm going to listen for His voice. If I think He's spoken to me, I'm going to test the word to make sure it was God who was speaking.

CHAPTER EIGHT

Prayer For the Sick and Hurting

A few years ago I saw an exposé on television about a woman faith healer who was causing quite a stir back east. She claimed to have had a near-death experience where God told her that she still had work to do, so He was sending her back to earth with a mission. Soon after, she began laying her hands on the sick and seeing miraculous results. Several medical doctors testified to the miraculous nature of the healings.

As part of the program, they videotaped one of her meetings held in a rented auditorium. The place was crowded with curious people and those seeking healings. In the front of the auditorium was an altar, a cross, and bunches of flowers. The woman asked people to come up to the front (just as countless Christians do at their weekly services across America) for healing while she sang "Amazing Grace."

In the interview that followed the service, the woman explained to the reporter that "the healings are a sign of God's love." She further stated that "God loves all people of all religions equally—Buddhists, Muslims, Hindus, Methodists, Lutherans, Pentecostal—all are valid avenues of knowing and experiencing God."

As she explained this, I was crying out to God, "Oh Lord, Jesus, do not let the enemy steal your glory! Send your power to the Church! I pray that...

> *...signs and wonders take place through the name of*
> *Your holy servant Jesus.*
>
> (Acts 4:30)

Since this woman did not heal by the authority of Jesus Christ, she is obviously a false teacher and healer and has not been sent by God.

Her words proved it.

Nevertheless, after the program I sat in my chair grieving, imploring God in prayer, saying, "Lord, pour out the miraculous in Your Church so that the Name of Jesus will be lifted up."

THE RELUCTANT PRAYERS FOR SICKNESS

There is a double standard in the Church concerning prayer. We pray confidently and often for courage, finances, comfort, wisdom, strength, patience, forgiveness, and emotional healings, but we are very reluctant to pray for physical healing.

When we are sick, we immediately call the doctor first; we are reluctant to ask for prayer. The Church has concentrated on the spiritual aspects of a person's life and has permitted science almost exclusive domain in dealing with the physical body.

Yet, when we examine the ministry of Jesus, it is easy to see that He dealt with both the physical and spiritual problems of people.

Generally, the Church has not emphasized praying for the sick. Therefore, into this vacuum has rushed a variety of false solutions such as New Age healings, eastern spiritualists, hypnosis, biofeedback, and meditation. In our day, God has presented the Church with a great opportunity and challenge to demonstrate the biblical truth of God's power to heal in spirit, soul, and body.

As Christians, we believe that all disease and suffering can be traced to the fall of Adam and Eve. Since we trace sickness and disease to the fall, we believe that Christ's death and resurrection changed the hopelessness of disease, emotional problems, and mental illness.

Most Christians will not deny that God may do miracles, but they become less confident when confronted with these two questions:

- How often can we expect supernatural intervention for divine healing?

- Is there really hope for healing in this life, or is our only hope for an ultimate healing in Heaven?

My sincere belief, based upon the Bible, is that as Jesus works through us, we should be expecting and experiencing far more healing and deliverances than we are. I came to this conclusion because Jesus revealed God's heart to us through His Word. God communicated His mercy and desire to heal diseases through Jesus' words and deeds. Jesus told us in John 5:19 that He said and did only what the Father told Him.

In the Gospels, Jesus performed 41 healings; 40% of the narrative verses deal with Jesus healing people. In fact, the ministry of Jesus centered on preaching the Kingdom of God and healing the sick!

We are exhorted in scripture to be *"imitators of Christ"* (1 Corinthians 4:16; Ephesians 5:1). That means Jesus should be our model for life and ministry. Therefore, we cannot ignore Jesus' healing ministry, nor His healing ministry through His disciples.

Many Christians resist divine healing because they have been exposed to poor models, false teachers, or false preachers. But remember, Jesus warned us that false teachers would work miracles and healings to try to deceive the elect (Matthew 24:24). The woman discussed at the beginning of this chapter is a good example of this. I believe the enemy uses these false teachers and preachers to discredit the authentic work of the Holy Spirit. Christians then become leery of the miraculous as they relate much of it to phoniness, fraud, and charlatanism.

PRAYING FOR SICKNESS—OUR COMMISSION

But the fact remains that Jesus not only healed the sick but He trained His twelve disciples, then the seventy, to do the same.

> *And He called the twelve together, and gave them power and authority over all the demons and to heal diseases. And He sent them out to proclaim the kingdom of God and to perform healing... Departing, they began going throughout the villages, preaching the gospel and healing everywhere.*
>
> (Luke 9:1–2, 6)

> *Now after this the Lord appointed seventy others, and sent them in pairs ahead of Him to every city and place where He himself was going to come. And He was saying to them... "Whatever city you enter and they receive you, eat what is set before you; and heal those in it who are sick, and say to them, 'The kingdom of God has come near to you.'"*
>
> (Luke 10:1–2, 8–9)

After reading these scriptures, does it not seem obvious that Jesus was training eighty-two people who could minister in His place? In Jesus' commission to His disciples in Matthew 28:18-20, He tells them,

> *Go therefore and make disciples... teaching them to observe all that I commanded you.*

Nowhere in these verses or in any other are we told that when Jesus said "all," He meant everything except praying for the sick. In fact, in a parallel verse, Mark 16:17-18, Jesus includes laying hands on the sick with His commission.

A disciple is someone who becomes like their teacher. The final product (the disciple) is similar to the original (the teacher). Jesus expected His disciples to train others who would train others to do His works down through the centuries.

Jesus was and is commanding His disciples to train men and women to do as He had done. That is exactly what they did and is exactly what we should be doing.

PRACTICE HEALING PRAYERS

All through the book of Acts, we see Jesus' disciples healing the sick and the Holy Spirit using these healings to open the hearts of the unsaved to the Gospel. As in Jesus' ministry, the physical healings gave His followers an opportunity to preach the Gospel (Acts 3; 8:4–7; 9:32–35, 36–42; 14:8–10; 28:7–10).

Praying for the sick was taught to new converts into the second and third centuries. Iraneus, who lived in Gaul (198 AD), testifies to physical healings that often led to conversions.[3] Gregory of Nyssa (335–395) writes that oil was given to Christians so they would pray for their sick relatives, friends and neighbors. He also states, "Healing is the main door through which people come to a knowledge of the truth."[4]

It is my belief that physical healings and other miraculous signs should accompany the preaching of the Gospel. These signs and wonders serve as a validation of the Gospel and of God's power. Paul reminds the Corinthians:

---

[3] Kelsey, Morton T. Healing & Christianity. Fortress Press, March 1, 1995.

[4] Graham, Rochelle; Litt, Flora; Irwin, Wayne. Healing From the Heart: a guide to Christian healing for individuals and groups. Wood Lake Publishing, 1998.

And when I came to you, brethren, I did not come with superiority of speech or of wisdom, proclaiming to you the testimony of God. For I determined to know nothing among you except Jesus Christ, and Him crucified. I was with you in weakness and in fear and in much trembling, and my message and my preaching were not in persuasive words of wisdom, but in demonstration of the Spirit and of power, so that your faith would not rest on the wisdom of men, but on the power of God.

(1 Corinthians 2:1–5)

When Paul preached the Gospel of Jesus Christ, he expected a demonstration of God's power to accompany His preaching—including physical healing.

Far too many Christians let their faith rest on the wisdom of men. They base their beliefs on the theologies of men who state that miracles died off with the Apostles. Considering Jesus' command to train disciples in "all" that He had commanded, it seems obvious that we still have an obligation to do the works of Jesus. As we proclaim His message, it should be accompanied by a *"demonstration of the Spirit and of power."* In 1 Corinthians 4:16–20, Paul tells them,

Therefore I exhort you, be imitators of me. For this reason I have sent to you Timothy, who is my beloved and faithful child in the Lord, and he will remind you of my ways which are in Christ, just as I teach everywhere in every church. Now some have become arrogant, as though I were not coming to you. But I will come to you soon, if the Lord wills, and I shall find out, not the words of those who are arrogant but their power. For the Kingdom of God does not consist in words but in power.

In verse 16, Paul tells the Corinthians to imitate his life, to practice their faith as he did by preaching the Kingdom of God and doing the works of Jesus, expecting a demonstration of God's power. Paul tells us that those who practice the faith that he practiced would manifest supernatural power. Paul evaluated a person's anointing and ministry by the Kingdom power exhibited through his or her life.

I graduated from a respected seminary, yet never heard anyone talk like Paul. Today we evaluate those in ministry by their oratory skills, graduate degrees and writing abilities. But Paul did not care how capable a communicator they were, or how learned they were—he only wanted to know if the Holy Spirit's power was manifested in their ministry.

The Church in America is filled with too many words but too little power.

Too few Christians are taking Jesus' words seriously, stepping out in faith, and praying for the sick and hurting.

That is why there is very little miraculous healing power being manifested in our churches today.

Paul expected supernatural healings to take place in the Church. He tells us that there are to be gifts of healings (1 Corinthians 12:9, 28) and miracles in the Church (verse 10). Nowhere in Paul's writings or in any other New Testament writings are we told that these healings and signs would cease. While some Christians believe this, their ideas are based on presuppositions and systematic theologies, not Scripture.

Show me one Scripture that says, 'After the Apostles die, the Church is to stop expecting signs, wonders, and healings.'

Shortly after Pentecost, the new Jerusalem church found itself facing fierce opposition. The Apostles were thrown into prison, brought before the Jewish leaders, and warned not to speak about Jesus. Soon after, they were released from prison and gathered the church together to pray about the threats of the Sanhedrin—a prayer recorded for us in Acts 4. Let us look specifically at verses 29-31:

And now, Lord, take note of their threats, and grant that Your bond-servants may speak Your word with all confidence, while You extend Your hand to heal, and signs and wonders take place through the name of Your holy servant Jesus." And when they had prayed, the place where they had gathered together was shaken, and they were all filled with the Holy Spirit, and began to speak the word of God with boldness.

Does this not describe what could be termed a second Pentecost?

God's Spirit was poured out so powerfully that even the building shook!

Wouldn't it be safe to say that God must have been pleased with their prayer?

And what did they pray?

They prayed God would grant His bondservants the ability to speak God's Word boldly and that signs and wonders would take place as they ministered in Jesus' Name.

Who are the bondservants mentioned here in Acts 4? All who were gathered together with the apostles. Therefore, wouldn't it be right to conclude that all who were in the Church could be referred to as bondservants?

Clearly, God was pleased with their prayer, and He made sure these Jerusalem Christians knew it, as well as all Christians who would pray this type of prayer down through the centuries. We have all been called to speak boldly for Christ and to minister in His name.

As we do, we should expect to see miraculous signs and wonders.

FOLLOW THE APOSTLES— NOT FALSE THEOLOGIES

In Acts 6:8 we are told that Stephen (not one of the 12 apostles) was *performing signs and wonders* among the people of Jerusalem.

In Acts 8, Philip (not one of the 12 apostles) was doing miraculous signs and healing the sick in Samaria.

The pattern is clear.

The ministry of Jesus and His Apostles was to be taught and passed on to their disciples who were to pass it on to others from one generation to another.

The Apostle Paul exhorted the Philippian believers to practice what they had…

> … *learned and received and heard and seen in me.*
>
> (Philippians 4:9)

Paul tells Timothy to pass on what he had…

> …*heard from me in the presence of many witnesses, entrust these to faithful men who will be able to teach others also.*
>
> (2 Timothy 2:2)

The process seems very clear.

Paul's ministry (Jesus' ministry) was to be passed from one generation to the next.

How can some Christians believe that Paul was not telling the Philippian church and Timothy to preach the Kingdom of God and to pray for miracles? There can be doubt only if they come to the Bible with presuppositions concerning what God can or cannot do. If believers come to the Bible without the presuppositions and systematic theologies taught to them concerning praying for the sick, they will pray for the sick because they will naturally assume that is what they are supposed to do.

I believe this is why there are more physical healings in third-world countries. They just do the works of Jesus and His disciples in a childlike faith and obedience.

American Christians have swallowed man's wisdom; we act like we have God figured out. We think we know what He will do and when He will do it and how He will do it. If God dares to move outside the parameters we have set up, we say, "Obviously that cannot be God."

What absolute arrogance permeates the Church of Jesus Christ in America!

In John 20:21 Jesus told His disciples,

> *As the Father has sent Me, I also send you.*

You and I have been called to continue the ministry of Jesus—including praying for the sick. As Christians, the Spirit of God is living inside of us, and God desires His power be released through us into the world around us.

Paul says we are Christ's ambassadors (2 Corinthians 5:20). We are literally the ministering hands of Jesus in our family, church, city, and world. In John 14:12, Jesus said,

> *Truly, truly, I say to you, he who believes in Me, the works that I do, he will do also.*

In my opinion, there is little power in the Church in America because there is little faith—the faith that would step out boldly and pray for seemingly hopeless situations.

More often than not, when we are faced with a crisis or hopeless situation, Christians in America look to worldly wisdom first before seeking God.

FAITH AND THE HEALING PROCESS

Anyone reading the New Testament can see how important God views faith. In Hebrews 11 we read,

Without faith it is impossible to please Him.

Jesus told us that miraculous things would be accomplished through faith (Mark 11:22-24).

Paul says, in Galatians 3:5,

Does He who provides you with the Spirit and works miracles among you, do it by works of the Law, or by hearing with faith?

Only our faith in God produces miracles.

Thankfully, we do not need much faith to be used by God in the supernatural. If only we have a tiny mustard seed of it, Jesus tells us,

Nothing will be impossible to you.

(Matthew 17: 20)

The faith to believe, pray for the sick or pray for the miraculous is nothing more than childlike faith and trust in the loving character of our heavenly Father.

It is so simple we miss it.

Christians think there has to be more, but our part is simply stepping out in faith and praying for the sick when the opportunity arises. It is my belief that the Church would be experiencing a significant increase in physical healings if people were taught to pray for the sick.

I will never forget the first time I experienced the Lord do a supernatural healing as I laid hands (simply because I knew we are commanded to) on a brother dying from cancer. Dan had been sent home to die by the doctors. They had given him approximately two weeks to live. I remember phoning his wife and gently asking her, "Do you mind if I pray for your husband?" Of course I felt inadequate and full of doubt, thinking, "Even if she says 'yes,' this wont do any good. The doctors have already said the man is going to die."

When I walked through the door, Dan was lying on the front room sofa, too weak to even sit up and shake my hand. I remember praying, "Lord, this man doesn't have much longer to live unless you do some-thing." When I looked closer at Dan, what little faith I had all but disappeared. Nevertheless, I suggested that we pray for a while.

Dan's wife and I knelt down and interceded for Dan's healing. Finally, I knelt down beside Dan and laid my hands on him, praying for a healing. There was no electricity, heat, or tingling. Neither of us felt anything. I remember asking Dan after I prayed, "Did you feel anything?" He answered honestly, "No, not really."

But as Dan testified later, from that moment he began to get better.

That night he ate for the first time in many days, and he kept the food down (up until this time he couldn't eat because the cancer had spread to this throat and stomach).

A few days later he took a short walk, which soon turned into longer walks, which led to him going back to work.

When I walked into Jack's hospital room, he was hooked up to several monitors and just looked terrible. Jack had suffered a severe heart attack and I had come to pray for his healing. I laid my hand on Jack's chest and said a little prayer and left. The next day when I returned Jack was standing next to the window in the hospital room. "Pastor," he shouted, "yesterday when you prayed for me God did something. I feel wonderful!"

Diane came forward on a Sunday morning. She had been told by several doctors that she had cervical cancer that had spread all over her abdomen. When she told me all that the doctors had told her, what little faith I had vanished. But because our Lord commands us to pray for the sick, I prayed for her healing. The Lord caused the cancer to go into remission, but the doctors refused to believe it. They had her go through one test after another and were totally baffled by test results.

The important lesson to be learned from these experiences is that God is the One Who does the healing. Our job is simply to be obedient and pray for the sick. A willing servant and obedient prayer is all the faith the Lord needs to accomplish His supernatural will.

The questions when praying for the sick are not, "Does this person I am praying for have enough faith to be healed?" or, "Am I able to whip up enough faith to pray effectively?" Rather, the true questions are, "Can I trust God with my life and the lives of others?" and, "Am I willing to be totally open to His love and ministering to and through me?"

True faith—the faith that produces miracles—is not rooted in works, in one's ability to believe, or in positive thoughts or fervent claiming. True faith is trusting Jesus, not our own abilities or knowledge. Faith is a willingness to commit ourselves to His ministry, what He has called us to do, and to open ourselves totally to His love, His ministry through us.

This type of faith will never disappoint (Romans 5:5), regardless of the outcome of the prayer—whether someone is healed in this life or not. We must believe that when we pray God listens and ministers to those we are lifting up to Him.

When my son was little and came running up to me, crying with his hands raised, I always lifted him up and loved him the best I could. Andrew had 100% confidence and trust that whenever he needed my love and attention, I'd give it to him.

He was right.

This is the kind of faith and trust you and I need to have in our Lord Jesus Christ.

I do not believe there is an unqualified entitlement or promise that everyone will be healed in the Bible. But, I do believe that if we consistently pray for the sick we will experience an explosion of physical healings in the Church.

Dear Brothers and Sisters, do you have enough faith and trust in God to be obedient and pray for the sick, leaving the rest to God?

Do you have enough faith to let others pray for you, knowing that our Lord will always love you when you come to Him in need?

My hope and prayer is that each of you reading this chapter will step out in faith and begin to do one of the works that Jesus has called you to do: Pray and lay hands on the sick in your sphere of influence in the name of Jesus.

What's the worst that can happen?

Those you pray for will sense the love and concern of Jesus through your actions whether they are healed or not. So...

- Be obedient.
- Be a disciple of Jesus.
- Be His hands to the world and minister to the sick around you.

CHAPTER NINE

Answered Versus Unanswered Prayer

PART 1

In the next two chapters I will discuss God's desire to answer our prayers and the question of unanswered prayer.

It is my contention that there is no such a thing as an unanswered prayer. What many Christians call "unanswered prayer" is really answered prayer—they just don't like the answer!

Answered prayer is important not simply because we receive what we ask for, but it is also important because it is proof that God is involved in our lives.

Answered prayer gives us evidence that God loves and cares for us. When our prayers are answered, it is unmistakable confirmation that God really is listening and that He truly is concerned about our daily lives.

Nothing verifies the truth about God in our lives more than answered prayer.

No one can argue with the testimony of answered prayer or try to tell you that God does not exist because God's miraculous power has touched your life.

My own testimony is that thirty years ago God intervened in my life because of prayer.

His intervention was unmistakable and irrefutable.

From that moment on, I have never doubted that there was a God. To do so, I would have to deny the obvious divine interventions in my life.

Is it any wonder Satan tries to keep us from praying?

Prayer substantiates God's existence and verifies God's word. Answered prayer glorifies our Lord in a way nothing else can. When God answers our prayers, we usually praise and glorify Him, verbalizing our faith and trust in Him.

ANSWERED PRAYER GLORIFIES GOD

Elijah could have prayed all day and night on Mount Carmel, but if God did not answer his prayer, no glory would have been given to God.

Jesus told us in John 15:7–8,

> *If you abide in Me, and My words abide in you, ask whatever you wish, and it will be done for you. My Father is glorified by this, that you bear much fruit, and so prove to be My disciples.*

Answered prayer glorifies God, and this passage seems to indicate that we bear fruit as our prayers are answered.

Further, answered prayer proves we are disciples of Christ. It is not merely the act of praying—what we say or how we say it that brings God glory—but the answer as well.

Based upon the Word of God, it is clear that Jesus Christ is committed to answering our prayers. Jesus said, "ask, seek, knock," but He also told us,

> *It will be given to you… you will find… it will be opened to you.*
>
> (Matthew 7:7)

God explicitly stated,

> *Call to Me and I will answer you.*
>
> (Jeremiah 33:3)

Nowhere in Scripture does it say, 'Call to Me and I shall teach you the skill of never receiving what you ask for.' Jesus never said, 'Ask and you shall learn perseverance by never getting what you ask for.'

Friends, the Gospel we preach, the Apostles preached, and Jesus proclaimed belongs in the miraculous. Take the supernatural out of our faith and it ceases to be alive.

Faith without miracles becomes nothing more than a "do and do not" religion. Prayer brings the miraculous power of God into the daily lives of Jesus' followers.

God has plainly committed Himself to answering prayer if we fulfill the three conditions that Jesus stated were imperative.

THREE CONDITIONS OF ANSWERED PRAYER

1. We must pray in the Name of Jesus.

> *Whatever you ask in My name, that will I do, so that the Father may be glorified in the Son. If you ask Me anything In My name, I will do it.*
>
> (John 14:13–14)

> *...Truly, truly I say to you, if you ask the Father for anything in My name, He will give it to you. Until now you have asked for nothing in My name; ask, and you will receive, so that Your joy may be made full.*
>
> (John 16:23–24)

Does this mean we must simply tack on the phrase "in Jesus' Name" at the end of all our prayers? Is this a magic phrase that assures our prayers will be answered?

Of course not!

When we pray "in Jesus' Name," we are submitting ourselves to the Lordship of Jesus Christ—His will for our lives. When we pray "in Jesus' Name," hopefully what we are praying for agrees with God's Spirit in that particular situation.

In 1 John 5:14–15, the Apostle John clarifies what praying "in Jesus' Name" means:

> *This is the confidence which we have before Him, that, if we ask anything according to His will, He hears us. And If we know that He hears us in whatever we ask, we know that we have the requests which we have asked from Him.*

Praying "in Jesus' Name" is simply finding the will of God for a particular situation and praying accordingly. We can be assured that if we are praying according to the will of God we will receive what we ask.

How do you find the will of God in a particular situation?

Start by asking this question: "Does my prayer agree with God's written Word?" If it does, then we can be assured that we are praying according to God's will.

Next, recognize that if you continue to pray about a situation over time, God will transform your heart, and your prayers will change to reflect His will.

Finally, you may need to seek godly counsel to decide how to properly pray (Proverbs 11:14). This is very important! So often Christians believe that God has spoken to them about a particular situation, when in reality, He has not. I have seen many Christians claim things "in Jesus' Name" that God would not endorse, so they end up praying for years prayers that seem never to be answered.

Clearly, the Lord will not respond to prayers that originate from selfish desires rather than the heart of God.

2. We must abide in Him and His Word. (John 15:7–8)

How do we abide in Christ?

1 John 3:24 tells us,

> *The one who keeps His commandments abides in Him, and He in him.*

We must be willing to read His word and assimilate its truths into our lives.

We must be willing to make a commitment to live according to the principles God has outlined for us.

In short, we must be obedient.

Our daily lives should reflect biblical values and principles. When we are striving to live this type of life before God, we have a promise from God that our prayers will be heard and answered.

3. We must have faith—a trusting belief in God's faithfulness.

Faith is probably talked about more than any other subject relating to prayer.

> *And Jesus answered saying to them, "Have faith in God. Truly I say to you, whoever says to this mountain, 'Be taken up and cast into the sea,' and does not doubt in his heart, but believes that what he says is going to happen, it will be granted him. Therefore I say to you, all things for which you pray and ask, believe that you have received them, and they will be granted you."*
>
> (Mark 11:22–24)

At the first reading of this passage, one might conclude that "If I pray for something and do not doubt, I can have whatever I want." Yet, if we are honest with ourselves, we know God is not going to give us everything we ask for—He loves us too much.

What if we ask for something that would ruin us?

Strain our marriage?

Cause us to suffer needless heartache?

As a parent I am not going to give my children everything they ask for because I love them. Therefore, there must be more to this passage than we first might realize.

We are told in Galatians 3:11 and Habakkuk 2:4 that "*the righteous man shall live by faith.*"

Faith in what?

God's faithfulness!

The assurance (belief or faith) that God is going to answer our prayers is grounded in God's faithfulness, not in our ability to believe!

Here's why:

If the emphasis to answered prayer hinges on our ability to have faith, our ability not to doubt, answered prayer becomes a work of man, something we can make happen.

If this were true, then prayer starts to sound very similar to the new age philosophy that says "We can create our own reality with the power of our minds!"

Let's not fool ourselves.

Without God's power no one is healed, no one is saved, the demonic forces are not pushed back—in short there are no mountains moved.

THE SOURCE OF FAITH

Jesus tells us in Mark 11:22, that we are to "have faith in God."

You and I are to trust in God's faithfulness, not in our own ability to think positively about a situation. The theme of Mark 11:20–24 and other similar passages is God's faithfulness to respond to us, not our ability to control the situation by our own discipline or determination.

When we remain constant, persevere in our trust of God's promises, and continue to pray according to His will, we will always experience answered prayer.

In Romans 4, Paul gives the example of Abraham as someone who exemplified the faith that Jesus was speaking about in Mark 11.

> *In hope against hope he believed, so that he might become a father of many nations according to that which had been spoken, "So shall your descendants be." Without becoming weak in faith he contemplated his own body, now as good as dead since he was about a hundred years old, and the deadness of Sarah's womb; yet, with respect to the promise of God, he did not waver in unbelief but grew strong in faith, giving glory to God, and being fully assured that what God had promised, He was also able to perform. Therefore it was also credited to him as righteousness.*

(Romans 4:18–22)

Abraham's faith was in God's faithfulness to fulfill His promises.

There were two occasions when Abraham tried to help God out, where his faith wavered. But eventually Abraham understood and trusted in the faithfulness of God. Abraham did not waver from this trust and *"it was also credited to him as righteousness."*

Many times Christians do not experience answered prayer because they simply give up. They doubt God's faithfulness!

Because of doubt, they do not receive what they have been praying for.

The prayer of faith, according to God's will, is always answered by our Heavenly Father.

CHAPTER TEN

Answered Versus Unanswered Prayer

PART 2

John, a member of our church, came to my office one day. He was extremely distraught over his wife's announcement that morning that she wanted a divorce. She had already seen a lawyer and was hoping the separation could be as amiable as possible.

John could not understand how his wife could turn her back on the commitment they had made before God. He was broken and devastated by her actions, not only for himself, but also for their two children.

Over the course of the next few days, John had many conversations with his wife but came away confused concerning why she wanted the divorce. John was willing to do whatever it took to rebuild the marriage, but unfortunately his wife was not.

She refused to talk to anyone: a mature Christian woman, her pastor, a counselor; she turned down all options. Her mind was made up.

Instead of giving up, John committed himself to intensely pray about his marriage. As his pastor, I joined with him in this cause, along with many other members of the church.

Despite our prayers, however, several months later the divorce was finalized.

But John persisted in his prayers!

"Surely God will soften my ex-wife's heart," he would tell me.

One day, John received a phone call informing him that his ex-wife was engaged to be married in two months.

John's faith was shaken.

He asked me the inevitable question: "Pastor, why didn't God answer my prayer? Wasn't this prayer according to His will?"

John's complaint concerning unanswered prayer is nothing new in spiritual history. From the earliest of times, God's people have been asking the same question.

> *How long, O Lord, will I call for help, And You will not hear? I cry out to You, "Violence!" Yet You do not save.*
> (Habakkuk 1:2)

> *I cry out to You for help, but You do not answer me; I stand up, and You turn Your attention against me.*
> (Job 30:20)

> *How long, O Lord? Will You forget me forever? How long will You hide Your face from me?*
> (Psalm 13:1)

Like Habakkuk, David and Job, Christians sometimes pray diligently for the resolution, the fulfillment of a deep desire, or deliverance, but no apparent answer comes. So they inevitably cry out to God asking why their prayer is not answered. Many Christians begin to question God's love for them and whether He is really listening to them.

What these Christians perceive as unanswered prayer becomes a profound problem for them because, as we have seen, the Bible specifically states that God answers prayer.

I have seen Christians get angry at God because they believe He is not answering them. They believe He's ignoring them.

As a result of this misplaced anger towards God, they stop their devotions, going to church, reading their Bible, praying, and they neglect fellowship with other Christians.

These individuals literally stew in a rebellious anger that leaves them wide open to temptation.

In this state, if an opportunity to sin comes along, they figure, "Why not? God doesn't care about me anyway! What does it matter?"

Unfortunately, I have seen this destructive attitude far too many times. To be honest, I have even experienced this attitude in my own heart towards God when my prayers were not answered according to my timetable.

FIVE HINDRANCES TO PRAYER

Dear Reader, how you and I perceive prayer—and how God answers prayer—are extremely vital areas to our spiritual survival. That is why the following information may be the most important spiritual truths in this entire book.

The Bible demonstrates that there are five definite reasons why God does not answer our prayers, or why our prayers may be hindered.

1. Reason One: SIN

*Your iniquities have made a separation between you and
your God, and your sins have hidden His face from you
so that He does not hear.*

(Isaiah 59:2)

Obviously, we all sin.

What is addressed here concerns the person who is willfully practicing sin. He or she knows what they are doing is wrong, but they refuse to do anything about their sin.

Make no mistake about it, this person's prayers are hindered before God.

The Bible contains numerous references that tell us that if we want to receive from God, we must obey His commandments.

*Whatever we ask we receive from Him, because we keep
His commandments.*

(1 John 3:22)

The prophet Malachi told the Israelites that the reason God was not responding to them was that they had stopped obeying His commands. The Israelites were marrying heathen women, not paying their tithes, cheating fellow Jews, divorcing the wives of their youth, and offering defective animals for sacrifice.

Because of sin, God had turned His face from them.

One Scripture that explicitly declares that sin will hinder our prayers is 1 Peter 3:7.

*You husbands in the same way, live with your wives in an
understanding way, as with someone weaker, since she*

is a woman; and show her honor as a fellow heir of the grace of life, so that your prayers will not be hindered.

This Scripture states quite clearly that if we sin in our relationship with our spouse, our prayers will be hindered before God.

Friend, if we want God to hear and respond to our prayers, we must be committed to turning away from sin and obeying His commandments.

Other Scriptures for further reference on this topic are: Isaiah 1:12–15; Psalms 34:15–16; Psalms 66:18.

2. Reason Two: IDOLS OF THE HEART

These men have set up in their idols in their hearts…
I will set My face against that man.

(Ezekiel 14:3,8)

Jesus told us *"Where your treasure is, there will your heart be also"* (Matthew 6:21). When we set an idol in our hearts—money, spouse, prestige, power, drugs, alcohol—we transgress the first commandment, *"You shall have no other gods before Me."*

When we transgress the first commandment, God sets His face against us and our prayers are hindered.

3. Reason Three: UNBELIEFs

James says that a man who is full of doubt (mistrust of God) should not *"expect that he will receive anything from the Lord"* (James 1:6-8). As we saw in Chapter Nine, faith is one of the conditions of answered prayer.

If that is so, then it stands to reason that unbelief would hinder our prayers before God.

4. Reason Four: SATANIC OPPOSITION

In Daniel 10:1–21, we see Daniel praying for the understanding of his vision.

Twenty-one days after he began praying, an angel appeared to Daniel and told him that he had been sent by God on the first day Daniel began praying, but demonic principalities kept him back for twenty-one days.

In 1 Thessalonians 2:18, we have an incident where Paul tells the Thessalonians that Satan had thwarted his plan to visit them. (Another similar Scripture is Romans 15:22.)

Therefore, God's Word shows us that it is very possible for our prayers to be hindered by demonic strongholds and influences.

We need to be open to praying against these demonic hindrances to prayer whenever the Holy Spirit reveals to us that there may be a Satanic hindrance to our prayers being answered.

But remember, Daniel's prayer was answered.

If we persist in prayer, Satan's strongholds and influences always must submit to the authority God has given us in Christ Jesus.

5. Reason Five: INAPPROPRIATE PRAYERS

The Bible tells us that the Lord will not respond to our prayers if they are inappropriate.

> *When the days were approaching for His ascension, He was determined to go to Jerusalem; and He sent messengers on ahead of Him, and they went and entered a village of the Samaritans to make arrangements for Him. But they did not receive Him, because He was traveling toward Jerusalem. When His disciples James*

and John saw this, they said, "Lord, do You want us to command fire to come down from heaven and consume them?" But He turned and rebuked them, [and said, "You do not know what kind of spirit you are of; for the Son of Man did not come to destroy men's lives, but to save them."] And they went on to another village.

(Luke 9:51–56)

The disciples wanted to pray to God and ask him to rain fire from heaven upon the Samaritans. This was obviously inappropriate, so Jesus rebuked them.

In James 4:3, the apostle tells us,

You ask and do not receive, because you ask with wrong motives, so that you may spend it on your pleasures.

If you have been praying diligently about a matter and have sensed a resistance from heaven, I challenge you to review your request and your motives to see if you have been praying appropriate prayers.

DO GODLY PRAYERS GO UNANSWERED?

What about those prayers that you believe to be in the will of God that seem to go unanswered?

What about when you have looked at God's Word and feel confident the Lord is pleased with your request?

What about the times you have sought godly counsel, and all agree your prayer is a godly one?

Yet, through it all, you receive no answer.

All you hear is silence.

Many become frustrated, discouraged and just give upon their intercession before God under these circumstances.

When you confront seemingly unanswered prayer, I want you to think of this anonymous quote that has stuck with me for many years:

"What many people perceive as unanswered prayer really is the problem of answered prayer."

(You may need to read that quote again to let it sink into your spirit).

The real issue here is that we Christians often lack knowledge or simply do not understand how God answers prayers.

As I stated in chapter 1, "What many Christians refer to as unanswered prayer is really answered prayer, they just do not like the answer."

Remember, my friend, the Lord always answers prayers.

When we pray according to His will and seek to live a sanctified life, the Lord must answer our prayers. There is no way around this biblical truth.

Prayers are not always answered as we would like, but they are always answered positively, never negatively.

Prayer, "in Jesus' Name," submitted to His will, is always answered positively.

> *Whatever you ask in My name, that I will do.*
> (John 14:13)

> *Ask and you will receive, so that your joy may be made full.*
> (John 16:21)

I do not believe our Lord ever answers our prayers in a negative way.

God is always positive.

Our problem is that many times it is hard to accept the positive answer that the Lord gives us. This is the problem of answered prayer.

God answers our prayers positively in four ways. What follows is not perfect, but it is my best attempt to understand how God answers our prayers.

Please understand, anytime we try to create a formula for how God works we will always fall short. Nonetheless, this description of how God answers prayer has been very helpful to me over the years as I have interceded and prayed for a variety of situations and individuals.

HOW GOD ANSWERS PRAYERS

Many believe God answers prayers in three ways: "Yes," "No," and "Wait." My personal opinion is that this view of prayer is not positive enough.

When it comes to the lives of His children, God is always thinking positively.

As you read through this, you still may be able to pick out "Yes," "No," and "Wait."

Nevertheless, I truly believe the Lord has showed me a better way to understand how He answers prayer.

1. God answers our prayers positively with a quick "YES."

This is the answer we all like—it's fast, quick, and easy.

This is the response from God we Americans like the best.

As quick as McDonald's fulfills our order for a hamburger, we put in our heavenly order and God answers us.

Years ago, my wife and I were asking the Lord to make it possible for us to take a vacation (we didn't have the money). Just a few days later a brother in the church gave my wife and I a gift of money. We had our answer to prayer quickly, and it was wonderful!

It is so exiting to pray for someone who needs a healing and then see that person healed right there on the spot or within a couple of days.

You can probably come up with examples from your own life of when God quickly answered your prayers. We all love the quick answers to our prayers because they involve little struggle, persistence, or commitment. I have never known anyone to complain that "God answered my prayer too quickly, and too positively."

Unfortunately, the theology of many Christians only has room for quick answers to prayer. Their theology says, "This is how God always answers prayer."

In my personal prayer life I have found that, more often than not, God answers my prayers not with a quick "Yes, David," but with one of His other three positive responses.

2. God answers our prayers positively with "Yes, here's the solution."

Years ago our little new church needed another place to meet on Sunday since the school auditorium and classrooms we had been using no longer were available. We asked the church to pray while we searched for a new building. Within a day or two of our search, the Lord provided us with the San Carlos Recreation Center. The director had helped start a church years earlier and was eager to have us use the facility.

Neither my brother, Mark (co-pastor), nor I liked the recreation center—it definitely was not what we had planned. We thought, "This couldn't possibly be God. The building has so many drawbacks."

The recreation center was very ugly, did not have heating or air-conditioning, the bathrooms were not kept up, and the acoustics were terrible! Believe me, there was not even one positive thing about this building except that it was available.

We continued to look for about two more months.

Finally, out of sheer desperation and having no other options, we signed a lease for the recreation center.

That recreation center proved to be the perfect place for us to meet for the next few years, especially considering some of the changes the Lord would make in our church.

Yet we almost missed God's provision, His solution for our church, because His answer to our prayer was not what we expected. There were some hardships to be sure; in the summer people would visit but seldom stay because of the heat. In the winter, visitors were driven away because our propane heaters gave off a terrible, gassy smell.

Despite these obstacles, looking back, we can easily see God's provision, although we almost missed it because the recreation center was not what we had planned. (To be honest, if it had been up to me, we would have missed God's provision. Praise the Lord—cooler and wiser heads prevailed.)

This entire experience made me wonder how many times I had missed God's answer to my prayers by assuming God never answered them. What I was calling "unanswered prayer" was already answered… I just did not like how God answered the prayer.

This is the problem of answered prayer.

Often, Christians miss God's answer to their prayers because it involves doing something. Frequently God says, "Yes, I hear your prayer. Here is My solution. Notice that you have a part to play."

God's answer sometimes requires us to actively make a change, a commitment, or to stop a certain activity. When we as Christians refuse to do what the Lord is asking, nothing happens.

Frequently, we are part of God's solution.

Over the years, husbands and wives have sat in my office and said, "I have prayed for my spouse for years and nothing's happening. Pastor, I am angry at God. He must not be hearing my prayer. I'm getting tired of hoping that God will respond to my pleas."

More often than not, as I speak further with these individuals, I discover that they are filled with anger, selfishness, and bitterness. What I believe God is telling them when they pray about their marriage is, "Yes, your marriage will change, but we have to start with you."

"Oh, no!" many respond. "Lord, You do not understand—my spouse is the problem!"

Unfortunately, nothing really happens in these marriages until they realize that God has told them where the solution lies.

But many do not like God's answer so they choose to ignore it.

At other times, our prayers seem to go unanswered because we ask God to do something that He has already guided or directed us to do ourselves. Many of those whom I have counseled in my office over the years have felt helpless about how they respond to people, situations and life in general. Others struggle to break the hold of various bondages that seemed to overtake them on a regular basis.

In almost every instance it has been fairly clear to me that the Lord is telling them to do something: to step out and trust God. Unfortunately, when they refuse to do what the Lord is asking of them, nothing changes in their circumstances.

It must be very frustrating for these people because they keep praying, "God, deliver me from this," "Please change this in me," or "God, please help me."

Yet God has already told them that if they want to change, there is something they have to do.

When we fail to do what God is asking, our problem never changes.

One of the ways God answers our prayers is by saying, "Yes, I hear you, and here's your solution. As you are obedient and follow through the solution I have given you, your prayers will be answered."

3. God answers our prayers positively with "Yes, in a little while."

This might sound like God telling you to "wait," but I prefer thinking of it as "yes" with a time delay. To me, God's "a little while" is almost as good as the Lord simply answering, "yes." Waiting for a short time is not a hardship for most of us.

But what about when God's "a little while" stretches on from months to years?

Friend, to endure these times you must know and understand God's heart. He is not on our timetable, but His time is always what is best for us.

Years ago, when I first heard this concept, I did not care for it because I was praying for something that I believed I could not live without.

But God kept showing me that He is never in a hurry and will always do things in His time, not ours. When God gave Abraham and Sarah a son, over twenty-five years had passed since God spoke the promise—Abraham was 100 and Sarah was 90! Hannah waited several years before she had her first child, Samuel. David prayed for years that God would vindicate him, deliver him from all his enemies, before it finally happened.

Often, God delays the answer to our prayers so He can develop character in our lives, qualities such as patience, endurance, trust and submission. By making us wait, God helps us to focus our eyes upon Him and not on circumstances, our own feelings, or what others may be telling us.

God desires for us to believe Him and base our faith strictly on what His word tells us, not what the culture, our friends, "the experts," or even our families are saying. As the writer of Hebrews explains, *"without faith it is impossible to please Him"* (Hebrews 11:6).

There are also instances where the Lord must wait until we or others are ready before He can fulfill our request. As I have grown older, I have thought back to some of the prayers I prayed when I was in my twenties and thirties. In retrospect, I am very glad God answered my prayers according to His timetable, not mine. Most of those prayers were realized in my life when I was mature enough to handle His blessing.

When our church first started in 1987, I remember how we prayed for God's Spirit to pour out upon us. If God would have moved then to the same extent He has moved in our church these last two years, we could not have handled the blessings! Over the last few years the church growth would have gone to our heads (especially mine). I would have been full of pride and arrogance, falsely believing that I had something to do with what God was doing.

Ultimately, God answered our prayers on His timetable when we were more spiritually prepared and ready to handle the blessings.

When my son was twelve months old, he would get into everything. The first thing he seemed to ask himself when he entered a room was, "What in this room can kill me?"

Instinctively, he seemed to always head for the one thing that would do him the most harm.

Naturally, as a good parent I wanted my son to learn how to use things in a responsible manner. But, I would have never given my one-year-old son a pair of scissors in hopes that he would learn how to use them properly after a few nicks and cuts.

So too with God.

Much of what we pray for is ultimately the will of God. It is just that our timing is off.

You may be praying for a good thing, but God knows you cannot handle the answer right now—giving your request to you at this moment would literally shipwreck your faith.

Remember, His time is always the best time for you!

Our requests for others are sometimes postponed because God is still working in their lives to prepare them for the fulfillment of our prayers. God is working as the result of our prayers, as He has promised, but we simply have not yet seen the fulfillment of our request.

When the Lord deems it fit in His wisdom to answer our prayer with, "Yes, in a little while," what is our usual response?

"No Lord, I cannot handle this another day! Please Jesus, not one more day—I need it now! I cannot possibly handle this situation any more. Please, Lord, fix it today. Change it today."

Does this sound familiar?

We often rant and rave before the Lord like spoiled little children.

If I have learned anything from my life it is this: God is not intimidated or moved by our assessment of our life situations. As an earthly father, I am not moved by my son's crying and whining when I take the scissors away from him.

In the same way, our heavenly Father is not moved by our repeated assertions of what we think is best for us.

Sometimes God must shake His head and say to Himself, "Dear son or daughter, you can kick, scream and pout all you want, but the time isn't right for you to see or experience the fruition of your prayer."

4. God answers our prayers positively with "Yes, I have heard you. I am going to bless beyond what you ask, even though you do not get what you want."

One beautiful example of this type of answer is the story of Lazarus in John 11. Lazarus' sisters, Mary and Martha, sent word to Jesus: *"Lord, behold, he whom You love is sick."*

The two sisters obviously believed that Jesus would come and heal their brother.

But, if Jesus would have come immediately and healed Lazarus, Mary and Martha would have missed out on one of Jesus' greatest miracles.

Jesus seemingly ignored Mary and Martha's plea to save their brother. They must have wondered why it took Jesus so long to come. Just like us, they did not understand why the Lord was not doing what they wanted, when they wanted it.

To them, it looked as if Jesus did not really care. In reality, He had something far better in mind than the sisters could have ever imagined.

In 2 Corinthians 12, we are told that the Lord did not heal Paul but instead gave him a greater gift of sufficiency and understanding.

There are times when the Lord answers our prayers by not giving us what we want so He can give us something even better. We may not see God's wisdom and love immediately, but over the long haul we will see and appreciate His timing.

This is not a "no" answer from God.

Rather, He is saying, "YES, I hear you, I love you, and I have something better for you. I'm not going to give you what you want; I'm going to give you something better."

I realize some of you reading this are having a bit of a struggle embracing what I'm saying because you've lost a child or a loved one. You prayed and believed for a miracle but none came and your loved one died. I can almost hear you saying, "This can't possibly be God giving me something better." My intent is not to discount your pain, as I've often seen it firsthand. Please stop and consider a few truths. First, you can't forget that your loved one is in heaven, a place beyond description. Even if they could they wouldn't want to come back. Secondly, I have heard countless testimonies of God doing great things in families and individuals because of a Christian's death, young or old.

The fact is God always has a purpose for what happens in our lives. It really does come down to perspective. When we have eternity in view, it really does change how we perceive and accept our loss.

When you were a teenager, if you asked your father for a ten-year-old car and he presented you with a brand new Ford truck, you would not say, "My dad did not give me what I want." You would scream, "Wow, my dad gave me more than I ever dreamed!"

Often, that is the case with God.

As I look back over my life, I am greatly relieved that God didn't give me every request that I asked of Him.

Ruth Graham once said, "If God would have given me every prayer, I would have married the wrong man seven times."

If I thought God would grant every prayer request without first reviewing my petition, I would almost be afraid to ask for things. I certainly do not want God to give me anything that would not be good for me. Do you?

At the beginning of this chapter I told you about John and his wife who divorced him. Even though the marriage was not restored, God has blessed John in all areas of his life. He would tell you, "God didn't give me what I wanted, but He gave me much more as He changed my life."

You may not get what you desire, but that does not mean your prayers are not answered. It only means that the Lord has something different planned. It may not be the easy way, but it will be the best way.

Please know that in your tough and difficult times, as you pray, God is working on your behalf. He goes ahead of you and prepares the way.

He strengthens you with His presence.

In short, God always answers your prayers.

The answer He gives you may not be precisely what you think you want. It may even be difficult at first, but in the long run, God's way is always best.

CHAPTER ELEVEN

Prayer and Fasting

Some time ago, in preparation to preach a message on fasting, I randomly called people in the congregation and asked them, "What is the first word that comes into your mind when you hear the word 'fasting'?"

The number one reply?

"Starvation!"

The dictionary defines starvation as "being deprived of food to the point of death."

Fasting is not starvation.

Americans have trouble with fasting because much of our lives revolve around eating. When we wake up in the morning, our first thought usually is, "What's for breakfast?"

By mid-morning, we start to think about what we will be eating for lunch, where we will be eating it, and with whom. Then, by mid-afternoon, we are thinking about dinner.

In our society, much of our socializing and communication revolves around eating together. Therefore, fasting has become a subject very few Christians really want to talk about.

Over the years, I have read many books about men and women who were used greatly by God. Their life stories have inspired me to actively pursue fulfilling God's purpose for my own life. As I read these books, one factor kept emerging over and over again: most of these men and women used by God practiced prayer with fasting.

When you read about most of the great revivals in spiritual history, you will frequently discover the mentioning of individuals who were praying with fasting. Martin Luther, John Calvin, Jonathon Edwards, D. L. Moody, David Branard, and Charles Finney all fasted with prayer.

THE UNPOPULAR NECESSITY

I believe fasting with prayer is unpopular with American Christians for two basic reasons:

1. Fasting has developed a bad reputation. Let's face it, there have been excesses surrounding this Christian discipline. Some have seen fasting as a works/righteousness theology, believing they can earn God's favor through fasting. Then there is the close association that fasting has with eastern religions and philosophies.

2. The western world holds the belief that we must eat three meals a day to be healthy.

If we do not eat regularly, we believe that our strength will be sapped and we will not perform up to our capacity. Also, the denial involved in fasting goes against the basic modern philosophy of, "If it feels good, do it."

However, the Bible indicates that fasting is a vital part of our Christian walk. The list of biblical people who fasted as they sought the Lord is impressive.

- Moses fasted before receiving the Ten Commandments (Exodus 34:28).
- King Jehoshaphat called a national fast to seek the Lord (2 Chronicles 20).
- Ezra sought the Lord through fasting (Ezra 8:21).
- Jesus fasted as He sought God in the wilderness before the start of His ministry (Luke 4).
- Paul and Barnabas prayed with fasting for direction before appointing elders (Acts 14:23).
- Daniel sought the Lord through prayer and fasting (Daniel 9:3).
- The church at Antioch fasted and prayed before sending Paul and Barnabas off on their first missionary journey (Acts 13:3).
- Elijah, Jeremiah, Esther, David, Mordecai, and Hannah are other biblical examples of people who sought the Lord with fasting.
- It surprises many people to find out that fasting is mentioned more than baptism in the Bible (77 to 75).

After all of this biblical evidence, we must come to the logical conclusion that fasting should be associated with any study on prayer. It is my belief that Jesus expected His followers would fast as they looked to God for direction, deliverance, strength, etc.

In Matthew 5:1 we read,

When Jesus saw the crowds, He went up on the mountain; and after He sat down, His disciples came to Him. He opened His mouth and began to teach them, saying...

From this verse to the end of Chapter 7 (three chapters) is what has become known as "The Sermon on the Mount," or "The Preaching of the Kingdom."

At the end of this sermon, in Matthew 7:24–27, Jesus says the following:

> *Therefore everyone who hears these words of Mine and acts upon them, may be compared to a wise man who built his house upon a rock. And the rain fell, and the floods came, and the winds blew and slammed against that house; and yet it did not fall, for it had been founded on the rock. Everyone who hears these words of Mine and does not act on them, will be like a foolish man who built His house on the sand. The rain fell, and the floods came, and the winds blew and slammed against that house; and it fell—and great was its fall.*

This parable describes two men who heard God's Word—but with one distinct difference: one acted on what he heard and the other did not. When tough times come ("in this world you will have trouble" John 16:33 NIV), if our lives are built on the firm foundation of God's Word, we will weather the storm.

On the other hand, if we turn away from the foundation of God and build our lives on the philosophies and values of the world, our lives collapse under pressure.

Fasting: an Option or an Expectation?

Jesus is warning His followers that they should seriously consider what He has just preached to them. In the midst of this message, Jesus says the following:

> *But when you give to the poor, do not let your left hand know what your right hand is doing.*

> (Matthew 6:3)

Jesus said "when" you give offerings to the poor. He didn't say "if." Jesus expected His disciples to give to the poor.

In verse five, Jesus says: *"When you pray…"* Here, as in verses two and three, Jesus expected His followers to pray. Because He assumed this, He gave them needed instructions concerning prayer (v.5–15).

After His instructions on prayer in verse 16, Jesus says, "Whenever you fast…" As with giving and prayer, Jesus expected His followers to fast! Clearly, the first eighteen verses of Matthew 6 indicate that Jesus expected His followers to give to the needy, pray, and fast.

And, since fasting is mentioned right after a teaching on prayer, can we not assume that Jesus expected it to be associated with prayer?

While Jesus expected His followers to fast, nowhere does He command or institute a fast, perhaps because fasting was very common during Jesus' time. The Bible speaks of the Pharisees fasting twice a week (Luke 18:12). We also know there were three public fasts per year: the Day of Atonement, the day before Purim (Esther 9:20–23, 31), and the ninth of Av (a month of the Jewish calendar), commemorating the fall of Jerusalem.

Fasting: Not a Command

Fasting is definitely present in both the Old and New Testaments, but there are no references commanding us to fast. In Leviticus 16:29, the Lord commanded the Israelites to "humble your souls" on the Day of Atonement. From the earliest times, the Israelites understood this to include fasting.

But since the Day of Atonement is no longer something God's people need to be concerned about, there is nothing in the Bible that commands us to fast.

Nevertheless, it seems that Jesus expected that His followers will humble themselves with fasting as they sought God's deliverance, direction, strength, and anointing.

WHAT IS A BIBLICAL FAST?

What does the Bible mean when it uses the word "fast"?

It means a voluntarily abstaining from food for spiritual purposes.

There are three kinds of fasts in the New Testament.

Fast #1: The Normal Fast

The first fast is called "the normal fast," and it is where one abstains from food but drinks liquid. This can be for various lengths of time—from one day to several weeks.

Fast #2: The Partial Fast

A partial fast is where one abstains from certain foods for a specific time (Daniel 1).

Fast #3: An Absolute Fast

The third option is an absolute fast where one eats and drinks nothing (Matthew 4:2; 1 Kings 19). Even though we have several examples of this type of fast in the Bible (i.e., Moses, Jesus, and Elijah), you should not try this fast because we cannot go without liquid for more than three days. Moses, Elijah, and Jesus were able to do this type of fast because God supernaturally made it possible.

If you are interested in further study on fasting, I would recommend you read the following:

a. *Fasting, a Neglected Discipline* by David Smith

b. *God's Chosen Fast* by Arthur Wallis

c. *Celebration of Discipline,* chapter 4, by Richard Foster. In Foster's book he gives a broader definition to fasting by including denial of any normal function (e.g., TV, eating meat, coffee, etc.) for spiritual reasons. But, when the Bible speaks about fasting, it is almost always referring to the abstaining from food.

FASTING FOR A PURPOSE

In the Bible, fasting is usually associated with seeking the Lord's help, strength, or deliverance in a crisis situation. There are a few instances where people fasted as a sign of great mourning. For example, David mourned the death of Jonathan with fasting (2 Samuel 1:11–12), but other than this and a few other scriptures, biblical fasting is usually associated with seeking God's supernatural intervention.

The next logical question we must answer is, "What is the purpose of fasting, and when is it appropriate?"

When I was twenty-two-years old, and a very new Christian, I had only one request of God: "Lord, please bring back the young woman who broke up with me so we can get married." I honestly believed that she would make a good wife and God had led me to meet her.

I desperately wanted her back, but she did not want anything to do with me!

Because I knew about people fasting in the Bible and had read biographies of godly men and women who fasted when they were desperate for God to move in their circumstance, it seemed pretty simple to me: "If I just fast and pray, God will give me what I want!"

I remember telling my mother, "I am not going to eat anything until God answers my prayer."

Of course, that was a stupid thing to say.

I was actually saying, "I am going to fast until God does what I want."

I was like the Jews in Acts 23 who made a vow not to eat anything until they had killed Paul. (I have always wondered, did these men die or did they break their vow and eat something?)

In my naïve, new Christian mentality, I began my fast—very determined to see it through to the end. As the days slipped by, the only thing that happened was that I grew very hungry. I realize now that God was not moved by my fasting because my only concern was my will, not His. God was trying to speak to me, but I was not listening. I wanted this girl back and I didn't want to hear that God had something better for me.

Jesus told us in Matthew 6 that when we fast, God is concerned about the motive behind the fasting. How easy it is to try to use fasting to force God to do exactly what we want.

Here is a spiritual key: God is not moved or intimidated by our sacrifices when they are done for selfish reasons. We can rant, rave, and go without food, but God will not be intimidated.

We cannot *make* God do anything.

In Isaiah 58, God tells Israel that their prayers and fasts were not heeded because they were done with the wrong motives. God asked the Jews in Zechariah 7:5, *"Was it for me that you fasted?"*

My first fast some twenty years ago was not centered on God's will being accomplished or for God's anointing, healing, or salvation but on my own will and desires. I was trying to twist God's arm by saying, "Look God, I'm really suffering down here. If You love me You'll do what I ask!"

I was like the little child who bites himself when he does not get what he wants. The child thinks, "If I hurt myself, then my parents will give me what I want."

This is exactly what I was doing!

This belief that fasting automatically moves God is a common error when people decide to fast with prayer. We must remember, fasting is not a way to try to manipulate God. It is not a magical spiritual exercise that enables us to receive what we want from God.

FASTING WITH GODLY MOTIVES

Fasting with prayer, when done to see God's will accomplished, is an expression of humility before God—just as raising our hands or kneeling in prayer expresses humility. These expressions are a physical statement of our dependency upon God.

When we humbly fast, we are saying to God, "Lord, I need your sufficiency, anointing, direction, wisdom, and strength to accomplish that which you have called me to do."

Fasting with prayer in and of itself is not humility—it is an expression of humility, just as kneeling or prostrating one's self before God is a sign of our dependence upon Him.

David said, "*I humbled my soul with fasting…*" (Psalm 69:10).

Fasting helps remind us of our constant dependence upon God because we are continually being reminded through our hunger, and when we see other people eating, why we are on a fast.

A study of the scriptures dealing with fasting reveals that when men and women fasted humbly, with the right motives, God always responded.

Throughout the Bible, as God's people prayed and fasted, God's power and sufficiency were released to meet their need.

- Daniel fasted and prayed for understanding, and he received it.
- Ezra fasted and prayed for protection and got it.
- Jehoshaphat fasted and prayed for deliverance and experienced it.
- Paul and Barnabas fasted and prayed for wisdom and manifested it.
- Nehemiah fasted and prayed for direction, and God gave it to him.

God's sufficiency, wisdom, and power were released in each of these instances where fasting was associated with prayer.

JESUS FASTED FOR POWER

In Luke 4, Jesus has just been baptized and is about ready to begin His ministry. In verse 1 we read,

> *Jesus, full of the Holy Spirit, returned from the Jordan and was led about by the Spirit in the wilderness... for forty days.*

After Jesus was baptized by John, He was full of the Holy Spirit. He was led into the wilderness where He fasted and sought the Lord for forty days (Matt. 4:2). After this forty days was completed, we read in Luke 4:14, *"Then Jesus, filled with the power of the Spirit, returned to Galilee."* He left *"full of the Holy Spirit"* and returned *"with the power of the Spirit."*

Do you think there is a difference between being "full" of the Holy Spirit and being "with the power" of the Holy Spirit?

Of course there is!

Jesus was full of the Holy Spirit, but He had to get alone with God so He could be in the power of the Holy Spirit. I believe that if we want God's power manifested in our lives, we must follow Jesus' example. God does not give His power to anyone on a consistent basis if they are full of pride or not seeking His will.

Why?

Because He cannot trust them.

The Bible tells us that God is "*opposed to the proud, but gives grace to the humble*" (James 4:6).

In 2 Peter 1:3 we see that God "*has granted to us everything pertaining to life.*" We also know that when we asked Jesus Christ into our lives He made His "abode" with us (John 14:23). His fullness entered our life.

Therefore, we all have Christ's authority, strength, power, and wisdom resident in our very being.

WALKING IN ANOINTING AND POWER

What separates Christians is their ability to exercise this power and anointing in whatever gifting God has given to them. One might have a gift for healing, another a calling to pastor, but the ability to minister that gift or calling is in direct proportion to the amount of God's power being released in their lives.

After His resurrection Jesus told His disciples to go and wait in Jerusalem until they received power from the Holy Spirit (Acts 1). On the Day of Pentecost, that power was made available to all believers for all time.

Friend, when was the last time you moved in the power of the Holy Spirit? Regardless of your theology concerning the Holy Spirit, try answering that question for your own life. When is the last time you shared the Gospel with someone and they became a Christian?

The question that has plagued me for years is this: "Where is the Lord's power in the Church?"

And just as important, "Where is the Lord's power in my life?"

I pray daily that I would be worthy of God's trust in giving me His power for ministry. As I do, I am beginning to understand that being in the power of the Lord revolves around sincere humility before God, coming to a place where we recognize that we truly cannot do anything without Him.

In Mark 9:14 and Matthew 17:14, Jesus comes down off of a mountain and sees His disciples trying to cast a demonic spirit out of a young man. The text tells us that there was a large crowd, and the scribes were arguing with Jesus' disciples. The problem was that Jesus' disciples could not cast the demon out. This confounded the disciples because they had done this type of thing before (Mark 6:7). They believed they were the chosen ones of Jesus and that God had given them the power to cast out demonic spirits.

Seeing a crowd gathering, Jesus cast the demon out. When Jesus had come into the house, His disciples began questioning Him privately. *"Why could we not drive it out?"*

Jesus replied, *"This kind does not go out except by prayer and fasting."* The reason they could not cast the demon out was because they lacked the power to do so.

They had been given the authority, they had been released to manifest this type of ministry, but they lacked the supernatural power.

I believe Jesus knew that His disciples needed to be humbled and admit their weakness, inability, and insufficiency. They needed to be reminded that it was not because of who they were that God's power was released through them, but it was wholly by God's mercy and sovereignty.

They were reminded in a very real way that, *"God is opposed to the proud, but gives grace to the humble"* (James 4:6).

I do not believe that God will consistently give His power to an individual unless they understand their position before Him. God will not give us the ability to exercise our gifting and callings with power if we are not humble before Him.

We all have authority to rebuke the enemy from our lives, but we need an anointing of power to do serious spiritual warfare.

You may have a calling as a pastor, but if you do not have an anointing of power you will never accomplish much for the Kingdom of God. Each one of us has gifting and authority, but unless we are anointed with God's power, we will never enter into all that the Lord has planned for us when He gave us our gifts and ministries.

Charles Finney, the great revivalist of the last century, a man mightily used by God, said, "Sometimes I would find myself in great measure empty of His power. Therefore, I would set apart a day of private fasting and prayer, humbling myself and crying out for help and God's power would return with all of its freshness."

My friend, God will not let you and I steal His glory! He desires that we continually be aware that it is His power and His authority that brings about change, salvation, restoration, and healing.

God works through humble people, and fasting helps to humble our souls before God.

WHEN AND HOW OFTEN?

You may be thinking, "Okay, Dave, I understand that fasting should be a part of my prayer life, but when, how often, and how long should I fast?"

Remember, the Lord Jesus never commanded or instituted any fast. Jesus simply expected that when His people understood their great dependency upon Him, they would fast. In the midst of their insufficiency in a crisis or desperate situation, when they wanted God to move mightily in their lives, family, church or community, Jesus expected they would humble themselves by praying with fasting.

How often? How long? What type of fast?

These are all personal decisions between you and God.

Of course, there might be instances where church leaders would call for a fast, but each person must still decide privately before God how they should respond.

Dear friend, fasting is an area of my spiritual walk with Jesus where I still have much to learn. But I think you can agree with me after reading this chapter that it is something we Christians should consider and practice to some extent.

If Jesus, Paul, Barnabas, and many other biblical heroes, plus countless mighty men and women of faith have fasted, is it not something that you and I should take seriously?

I want and need God's power and anointing in my life. If fasting helps to put my mind and soul in a better place to receive from God, then I am going to practice it.

But please, do not fast because of a feeling of religious obligation or guilt. Further, do not see it as a magical exercise to get something from God. Instead, fast because you love God and realize how much you need Him, how much your family and city needs Him.

I want to fast because I desire God's kingdom to come and His will to be done, and because I know that Jesus is *"the way, and the truth, and the life."* God's power must be released to break the strongholds that veil people's minds from the truth.

My prayer for each of you is that you will prayerfully consider how your prayer life can include the discipline of fasting.

CHAPTER TWELVE

Prayer Society

The years my brother Mark and I have preached scores of messages on the importance of prayer. We have repeatedly challenged our church to pray and attend our regularly scheduled prayer meetings during the week.

Frankly, the lack of response (especially years ago) was very frustrating for both myself and my brother. Of course, we knew that attendance at these prayer meetings was not the sole measure of the church prayer life, but it still was disturbing.

We understand that people are very busy in our hectic society and that it is difficult to dedicate a specific time each day to pray. But if we cannot find the time to pray, then something is seriously wrong with our priorities.

Each time Mark or I would teach on the subject of prayer at our weekend services, we would see a temporary increase in attendance at these prayer meetings, but the increase was always short-lived.

People would also be inspired by the Holy Spirit to commit themselves to daily times of prayer at home, but too often these good intentions were fleeting.

Studies have shown that people remember less than one-fifth of what they hear in a sermon. Personally, I believe it may be even lower than that. It has also been shown that if people do not practice what they hear, they forget what they hear in about ten days. So, if we are not practicing prayer, in all probability within a few weeks of hearing a sermon on the topic, most Christians will revert back to lives without prayer.

This is frustrating and should serve as a warning for any preacher. If you want your message to change lives, you had better be a man of prayer. Prayer not only anoints the teacher but also anoints and prepares the hearts of those who will be listening.

Hopefully, by this point in this book you would agree with me that prayer is the single most important activity in our Christian life. Prayer is the key to relationships, knowing God's will, having intimacy with God, experiencing peace, wisdom, strength, anointing, and emotional wholeness. Therefore, you can see why I am burdened that God's people become men and women of prayer.

It is apparent to me that we in America will never experience revival in the Church, reap a harvest of souls, or see righteousness come to our cities without Christians falling to their knees and crying out to God.

Each of us must make prayer a priority if we expect things to change in our American society.

I am constantly reminded that Jesus' disciples did not ask Him to teach them how to preach, teach, evangelize, or do miracles. What they asked Him was, "Teach us to pray!"

Obviously, they understood that prayer was the source of Jesus' anointing and His ability to do God's work.

That is why, today, the Church's seeming lack of prayer troubles me deeply.

One week after finishing a series of messages on prayer, our family attended a reunion in Palm Springs. My parents rented a beautiful house on a golf course, and we stayed there for a week. Every morning I would get up early to pray while walking around the golf course. I was tremendously burdened that we as a fellowship would never impact our city for Christ the way we envisioned unless we became a people of prayer.

I kept asking God, "How can we encourage prayer and experience a dramatic increase in prayer in our church?" I knew there had to be an answer and that God would surely give it to me if I prayerfully persisted in my request.

One morning as I finished my prayer walk and was sitting on the patio reading my Bible, the Lord gave me the answer: we were to begin a Prayer Society at the church. Each member would pledge themselves to pray a minimum of time each week and practice basic Christian disciplines weekly for six months. Each member would be sent a prayer list compiled at the church office every two weeks so they could regularly pray for these specific petitions. A recent prayer list I sent to our Prayer Society included: prayer for all of the church staff with special prayer for the worship team, an anointing on song writing, prayer for a neighboring church that was searching for a new pastor, prayer for Christian teachers in public and private schools, prayer for numerous ministries at the church, and finally, prayer for two church children who were seriously ill.

After the six month commitment was over, we would hold a special, free appreciation dinner for the Prayer Society at a local restaurant, or cater dinner at the church, honoring them and encouraging them to sign up for another six months. In addition, I would preach a special message on prayer every six months to encourage others to enroll.

When I ran this idea past my brother and the rest of the church staff, I received strong agreement and confirmation. I decided to launch the Prayer Society as soon as possible.

We decided on five specific pledges that each Prayer Society member would commit themselves to for six months.

The pledge reads as follows:

I, _____, by affixing my signature hereto do pledge to commit myself for six months to these objectives:

1.   Praying a minimum of two and one-half hours each week. (This is the combined amount of time spent in all facets of one's prayer life.) [Most pray 30 minutes a day, 5 days a week or come to one of several of our prayer meetings to fulfill their pledge.]

2.   Attending church regularly.

3.   Supporting the church's ministry through my tithes and offerings.

4.   Striving for holiness and obedience to God in my daily life.

5.   Praying regularly through prayer lists that will be compiled at the church office every two weeks.

_____ Date _____ Member

_____ Witness

Several weeks later I preached a message on our responsibility to pray and intercede. I closed the message by challenging the congregation to prayerfully consider joining the Prayer Society. I explained what would be expected and that they could sign up by meeting me at the church five days later on a Friday night.

I did not take signups for five days because I only wanted people who were serious about prayer. I figured that by asking them to come to church on a Friday night to sign up, it would separate the serious from the emotionally stirred.

When Friday night came, one hundred and forty adults showed up!

I was shocked and even more convinced that the Prayer Society was something that God had initiated. Over the years we've changed how we do sign-ups. Approximately every six months I preach a message on prayer and challenge the congregation again to become a Prayer Society member. We have a flyer in the church bulletin, which they fill out and sign, and then at the end of the service, they bring their signed pledge up to the front and lay them on the stage.

When people sign up, I give them various prayer tips that I have compiled to help them pray. Many of the new members have no idea of the challenge and effort that will be required to fulfill their six-month commitment.

I also explain that some of them might not live up to their commitment in any given week. If that happens, I instruct them to ask God to forgive them, then start anew. I warn them that the enemy will try to use their failures to pray at any particular time as a way to trick them into giving up on their commitment altogether. I make sure that they understand that the entire purpose of the Prayer Society is to help increase our prayer lives, not to put us under condemnation. They simply needed to ask God to forgive them and start again the next day. One of the great things about God is that yesterday is forgotten. It's what we do today that counts (Lamentations 3:22–23).

Those first six months there was an excitement and expectation as to what would be the result of this concentrated prayer. I am not exaggerating when I tell you that during the first year of the Prayer Society, the overall ministry of our church doubled. There were other factors involved (for example, moving into a new facility), but these other factors do not account for the ministry explosion that took place.

The Spirit of God's love permeated our church.

- Our Sunday morning attendance more than doubled.

- Within one and a half years our new facility was too small.

- We reached our goal of ministering to one thousand children and youth each week.

- We began to baptize people at a rate we had never experienced.

- Countless people came up to Mark and me, testifying that our messages of late had really been anointed.

- Our Small Group leaders noticed an increase in attendance and commitment.

- In all areas of ministry the measurable results were astounding.

One of the things that the Prayer Society prayed for regularly was the full-time staff. This meant we had more people committed to praying for us than ever before. Personally, I noticed an increase in power and anointing in every area of my ministry and health.

For years I was known as a fairly sickly person who was always fighting something. The year before starting the Prayer Society I had nine different, distinct illnesses.

The year after we began the Prayer Society, there were far fewer times that I stayed home because of illness.

Was this simply a coincidence?

I doubt it.

Prayer was energizing our church. Our ministry was exploding. We now refer to our Prayer Society as the most important ministry in the church.

Scores of people in our church are developing a prayer life as a result of their commitment as Prayer Society members. By joining the Prayer Society, they started praying not only for the church but also for their own marriages, children, relatives, employees, employers, neighbors, direction, strength, etc. Imagine the impact these prayers are having on countless situations throughout our city.

One single mom told me, "Dave, I didn't think I'd ever have a meaningful prayer life. My schedule is just too busy." But since joining the Prayer Society, God has helped her to put aside thirty minutes in the mornings to be alone with Him. God has also helped her to learn how to pray while she works during the day. She prays while she washes clothes, sweeps the floor, drives her car, does the laundry, washes the dishes, etc. She prays for her neighborhood (which has numerous single moms), and has seen many families come to the Lord. Her three children have all accepted Christ, and God has opened their hearts to spiritual things as she has continued to pray.

Another successful middle-aged man testified that his life was so hectic that he never found time to pray. But after joining the Prayer Society, he began to make time for prayer since he had made a commitment to his church and to God. In keeping this pledge, he developed a discipline of prayer—something he always longed to do. He also noticed an increase in his ability to handle stress, make difficult decisions, relate to others with wisdom, and grow as a father and husband.

Overall, people testify that joining the Prayer Society has forced them to pray, which has resulted in a greater awareness of God, His will, and His leading. Prayer has released God's power into the situations in their lives.

One of the most exciting things to happen as a result of starting the Prayer Society is that other churches have started similar Prayer Societies! I believe the Lord spoke to my heart and told me that many who read this book will be moved by the Holy Spirit to begin Prayer Societies at their own churches.

If the Lord is speaking to you about this, please be obedient. Talk to your pastor about launching a Prayer Society. As you do, God will release His mighty power and anointing upon your church, local community, and city in an unprecedented manner. At this writing we have over 1,000 members in our Prayer Society. Imagine one thousand people in one church serious about developing a discipline of prayer. Do you think this makes a difference? You bet it does.

If you're a pastor or church leader, I'd love to answer any questions you might have about this important ministry. Give me a call at our church (619-442-7728). If I'm unable to answer your call, I promise someone will.

CHAPTER THIRTEEN

Intercessory Prayer

Before we take two chapters and talk about how to develop a prayer life, let's remind ourselves of the importance of intercession. Intercession is when you place your prayer emphasis on others rather than self.

When we pray for someone, we become the conduit that brings God's power, influence and authority into their life, and circumstances.

The Bible is filled with examples of people who interceded for others before God:

- Moses interceded on behalf of the Israelites whom God was about to destroy (Exodus 32:11–14).

- Abraham prayed for the cities of Sodom and Gomorrah (Genesis 18:20–26).

- King Hezekiah interceded for the Kingdom of Judah (2 Kings 19:14–19).

- King David prayed for the people when a plague broke out among them (1 Chronicles 21:16–17).

- Daniel interceded for the Jews in captivity (Daniel 9:16).

- Jesus interceded for His disciples and the future Church (John 17).

- Paul interceded for the Church in Rome (Romans 1:9–10).

These passages are only a small fragment of scriptures that give us examples of God's people praying on behalf of others.

Jesus told us that we are the salt of the earth. Like salt, we are to give flavor to everything we touch. Salt was used as a preservative in the days of Christ, restraining food decay. The Church is God's preserving agent in the world and the main barrier to Satan's influence.

How can we be the salt of the world?

One way is through intercession. Prayer brings God's influence into the individuals and situations that confront us every day. Our major weapon to hold back the evil the enemy is planning for our churches, cities, and families is intercessory prayer.

The Bible commands us to pray for others:

> *First of all, then, I urge that entreaties and prayers, petitions and thanksgivings, be made on behalf of all men, for kings and all who are in authority, so that we may lead a tranquil and quiet life in all godliness and dignity. This is good and acceptable in the sight of God our Savior, who desires all men to be saved and to come to the knowledge of the truth.*
>
> (1 Timothy 2:1-4)

This Scripture clearly tells us that we should be interceding in prayer for others.

- In Colossians 4:3 and 1 Thessalonians 5:25, Paul urges us to pray for leaders in the Church.

- In Ephesians 6:18, Paul asks us to pray for all the saints.

- Jesus urged us to pray for laborers for the harvest (Matthew 9:38), and to pray for our enemies (Matthew 5:44).

I believe it is fair to say as Paul did in I Timothy 2:1 that the Lord would have us pray "on behalf of all men."

10 Truths About Intercessory Prayer

There are ten basic truths I have learned about intercessory prayer through the years, and in the rest of this chapter, I'd like to share them.

1. Intercession proclaims our dependence upon God Almighty.

When we intercede, we are admitting that without God we can do nothing (John 15:5). It then follows that nothing will change in any situation or person's life without His intervention.

We proclaim that Jesus is the answer (John 14:6), and that only God can break bondages permanently (Romans 6:6–7). Intercession proclaims that Christ has overcome this world (John 16:33); therefore His power, influence, and authority are sufficient for any circumstance.

Intercession gives testimony that the Lord answers prayer (Psalm 65:2,5) and is a proclamation of our total dependence upon God (His mercy, love, forgiveness, authority, strength, influence, wisdom etc.) in every situation.

Show me a person who believes that God can and will change circumstances, and I will show you a person who intercedes because that person recognizes their dependence upon God for their anointing and wisdom to minister in the Kingdom of God.

2. Intercession involves reminding God of His promises as we intercede for ind.ividuals and circumstances.

On your walls, O Jerusalem, I have appointed watchman;
all day and all night they will never keep silent. You who
remind the Lord, take no rest for yourselves; and give
Him no rest until He establishes and makes Jerusalem
a praise in the earth.

(Isaiah 62:6–7)

Who are these watchmen Isaiah is speaking about? They are the prophets God sent to His people.

In our day, who are these watchmen who watch over our cities?

I believe that you and I as Christians are the watchmen who must watch over our families, neighborhoods, cities, and communities. We are the ones who are standing on the walls as the main barrier that restrains evil from taking over.

As the watchmen, we have been called to intercession, to "stand in the gap before Me [God] for the land" (Ezekiel 22:30). As we stand in the gap (between others and God) interceding, God wants us to remind Him of His promises. Jacob, Samuel, Daniel, Solomon, Hezekiah, Moses, Nehemiah, Isaiah, and Jeremiah all reminded God of His promises (Genesis 32:11–12; Exodus 32:11–14; Nehemiah 1:5,8–10).

As you and I remind God of His promises during intercession, several truths become apparent to us.

a. We are reminded again of our desperate need for God to work in the situation or individual about which we are concerned.

b. As we review again His promises to us and others, faith is released in our lives. The Bible says that faith pleases God (Hebrews 11:6), and when faith is released or manifested, God moves mountains

(Mark 11:20–24). When we remind God of His promises, our faith is built up and releases God's power. I cannot say I understand how this works, only that God's power is released through faith.

Therefore, if we want to pray effectively for others, we need to be aware of God's promises and covenants with us. You and I must memorize Scripture as a priority in our lives so we can pray God's promises into our intercession for people, situations, or communities.

For example, if you are interceding for a young man who grew up in the Church and has fallen away, you could remind God of Proverb 22:6. When we *"Train up a child in the way he should go, even when he is old he will not depart from it."*

If you are praying for someone who is about to undergo surgery, you could pray Deuteronomy 31:8, reminding God that said He would never leave or forsake us, and that He would go ahead of us.

If you are praying for a spiritual awakening in your church, you could pray Luke 11:13, reminding God that He promised to send His Holy Spirit to us if we ask.

When you are praying for someone's salvation, you could remind God of 1 Timothy 2:4, which states that God "desires all men to be saved."

The scriptures we can use in our prayers are numerous. If you have not memorized many of God's promises, go to your local Bible bookstore and purchase a small pocket-sized book entitled *God's Promises.*

Start memorizing.

Begin to use God's Word in your intercessions for your family, neighbors, church, city, and nation.

3. Intercession opens doors.

The word "door" is used metaphorically in the Bible to indicate "an opportunity to preach the Gospel or enter into spiritual deliverance." When we pray for people and circumstances, God opens a door for the Holy Spirit to go into that situation, or person's life.

When this happens, power is released for deliverance, removal of strongholds, acceptance of the Gospel, etc.

> God opened a door for Paul and Barnabas to preach the gospel in Antioch (Acts 14:27).
> Jesus tells the church at Philadelphia that He had opened a door for them to minister in the face of slander and persecution from the Jews (Revelation 3:8).
> Paul asks the church at Colossae to pray that God would open a door so the Word would not only be preached but understood and believed (Colossians 4:3–4).

It takes prayers of intercession to open doors that the kingdom of darkness would like to remain shut.

As we pray, the Lord opens doors of opportunity in the situation we are praying about. For example, as our church prayed about our vision of ministering to 5,000 children and youth a week, God opened doors of opportunity just like He did when we were praying about ministering to 1,000. As we prayed, God gave vision and insight to our children's and youth pastors in developing new outreaches; He gave members of our church vision for starting various types of new ministries. All the barriers and strongholds that the enemy set before us to thwart our goals were eliminated by the intercession of the saints.

The doors (strongholds) that were shut against us were rammed open by our prayers.

The doors of opportunity may be as simple as your next door neighbor asking you about what church you go to, your children asking their friends to go to church with them, or a co-worker whose wife has just left him wanting to know if you would pray for him. These simple open doors could result in children and adults coming to a saving knowledge of Jesus Christ.

However it happens, whether the doors being opened involve a city council member who suddenly changes his vote, the children next door wanting to go to church with you, or a loved one suddenly becoming open to the Gospel, prayer will open doors of opportunity for us.

When I first became a Christian, I desperately wanted to be used by God. I began to ask God to give me opportunities to serve Him. I did not care what it was; I just wanted to be used. Almost immediately I became involved in leading Bible studies at a prison ministry, leading in the youth ministry at the church I was attending.

Friend, when you and I intercede, doors of opportunity are opened for ministry, healing, salvation, service, and deliverance.

4. Intercession involves bold persistence or perseverance (Luke 11:5–10; 18:1–14; Matthew 15:22–28).

When we intercede for individuals or circumstances, we must be willing to pray until the answer or deliverance comes. One reason Christians do not see results from their intercession is that they quit too soon, giving up praying when they do not see anything happening right away. Unfortunately, impatient Christians far too often are not willing to pay the price of prayer.

Make no mistake: intercession is work. It involves time and effort. Jesus told us that we are to keep praying until the answer comes (Luke 11:5–10).

5. Intercession desires the best for others.

As we intercede for others, we must honestly desire God's best for them. We must put aside all selfish desires concerning them and seek only God's will for their lives. This is not always an easy thing to do, especially when praying for loved ones or individuals whose lives deeply affect us.

For example, when a young woman becomes a Christian and is dating a young man who is unsaved, she might begin to pray that her boyfriend become a Christian. But that prayer probably has an element of selfishness because she does not want to break up with her boyfriend. True intercession would seek this young man's salvation even if it meant she needed to break up with him.

A Christian father spent years praying for his rebellious son who was into drugs and living a lifestyle leading to destruction. When praying for his son, the Father prayed two things: 1) that God would bring him home repentant and ready to change his life; and 2) that our Lord would save the boy from himself and keep him from getting arrested.

One Saturday morning as this father was praying for his son, the Lord spoke to his heart and showed him that his intercession for his son was based—in some degree—in selfishness. You see, this man was well known in his community, and if his son were to be arrested it would be in all of the papers. His son's drug use and rebellious lifestyle would be known to all, and his reputation would suffer. When the father recognized this attitude in his heart, he repented and began to pray that the Lord would do whatever was necessary to deliver his son.

Two days later his son was arrested.

The arrest was in all the papers, but when the father met with his son in prison, he was broken and repentant, asking his father to forgive him, and to let him move home to straighten out his life.

True intercession looks past our own individual needs and prays for God's will to be accomplished. It looks past our own views, desires, evaluations, and dreams and truly asks God to do what is best for that person or situation.

True intercession is not always easy, but if we truly love and are concerned about a situation, isn't it best to pray for God's will? When we trust God, we are never disappointed (Romans 10:11). God's thoughts and ways are often quite different than ours, but they are always best.

Pure intercession involves love that is willing to sacrifice one's life for a friend (John 15:13).

6. Intercession may demand that we be willing to be part of the answer.

We must be willing to say, "Lord, if You can use me to help bring about the change that I'm asking for, I'm available."

If we are not willing to make ourselves available to help bring about change, then we are not really serious about our prayer. We are like Pontius Pilate washing his hands and saying, "*I am innocent of this man's* [Jesus'] *blood*." He was not innocent. He was responsible, and so are we.

Too often we Christians pray for others and then wash our hands of the situation, thinking we have done our part. What we are saying to God is, "Lord, we are too busy to get involved. That situation is just too demanding and messy."

Friend, do not pray for the youth ministry unless you are truly willing to be a volunteer.

Do not pray for missions unless you are willing to give of your finances or send your children.

Do not pray for someone's financial need unless you are willing to ask God if there is something you can do.

> *If a brother or sister is without clothing and in need of daily food, and one of you says to them, "Go in peace, be warmed and be filled," and yet you do not give them what is necessary for their body, what use is that? Even so faith, if it has no works, is dead, being by itself.*
>
> (James 2:15–17)

We need to pray and intercede not only with our tongues but with deeds and truth.

> *Little children, let us not love with word or with tongue, but in deed and truth.*
>
> (1 John 3:18)

7. The Holy Spirit can intercede through us as we pray in an unknown tongue.

If the Lord has given you the gift of tongues, He expects you to use it for the edification of the Church (1 Corinthians 14:12). Paul also tells us that all spiritual gifts are given for the common good (1 Corinthians 12:7). Therefore, if you have been given the gift of tongues, use it to edify the Body of Christ through intercession.

The gift of tongues has been a great benefit to me in my times of prayer. After I have prayed all I can, but still feel burdened to intercede, I continue by using my prayer language. The gift of tongues has definitely increased the time I am able to spend in prayer.

In Romans 8:26-27 Paul tells us:

> *In the same way the Spirit also helps our weakness; for we do not know how to pray as we should, but the Spirit Himself intercedes for us with groanings too deep for*

words; and He who searches the hearts knows what the mind of the Spirit is, because He intercedes for the saints according to the will of God.

There are two things being said here:

1. The Spirit can intercede for us when we do not know what to say or cannot speak because we are overcome with emotion.
2. The Spirit can intercede according to the will of God because He obviously has the mind of Christ for the saints.

Some of our most powerful prayer times may be nothing more than simple sighs or weeping. We can be deeply moved by the Spirit to intercede for others who are in desperate need and so affected that all we can do is weep, groan or sit in silence before God. During these times of great emotional feelings, the Holy Spirit is still interceding through us even though we may not be verbalizing any specific thing.

Paul tells us that the Spirit can help in our weakness when we do not know what or how to pray. In these cases, it is my belief that the gift of tongues can be a tremendous blessing. As we pray in tongues we are literally praying the perfect prayer because we are praying "according to [God's] will" (1 John 5:14–15).

If you have been called to intercession, the gift of tongues can be of great benefit. This is not to say that someone who does not have the gift of tongues cannot be a great prayer warrior, only that having a prayer language can help us intercede. I personally know many who spend hours with the Lord each week who do not have the gift of tongues. But, it has been my experience that tongues makes it easier to increase one's prayer life. If you do not have the gift of tongues, why not ask the Lord if this is something He would have for you to help in your prayer life?

8. Intercession may include identification with the sin, suffering or joy of others.

One example of this type of intercession is the prayers of Ezra and Nehemiah after they were informed about the condition of Jerusalem.

> *When I heard about this matter, I tore my garment... and I sat appalled until the evening offering... I arose from my humiliation... and I fell on my knees and stretched out my hands to the Lord my God; and I said, "O my God, I am ashamed and embarrassed to lift up my face to You, my God, for our iniquities have risen above our heads and our guilt has grown even to the heavens... Now, our God, what shall we say after this? For we have forsaken your commandments.*
>
> (Ezra 9:3–6, 10)

> *Let Your ear now be attentive... open to hear the prayer of Your servant which I am praying before You now, day and night, on behalf of the sons of Israel Your servants, confessing the sins of the sons of Israel which we have sinned against You; I and my father's house have sinned.*
>
> (Nehemiah 1:6)

Both Ezra and Nehemiah were righteous men, but in their intercessions they identified themselves with the sins of their contemporaries and forefathers. When we ask God to pour out His mercy and compassion on others, let us take the example of Ezra and Nehemiah and identify with the sins of those for whom we are praying.

This is not that difficult because apart from Christ we all have the potential for evil lurking within us. Apart from Christ, and given the right circumstances, all of us could commit any sin in the Bible.

Paul said,

> *I find then the principal that evil is present in me, the one who wants to do good.*

(Romans 7:21)

We can all identify with sin because we *"all have sinned and fall short of the glory of God"* (Romans 3:23).

When we pray for others, it pleases God if we humble ourselves and recognize that we are no better than anyone else (Romans 12:3). We then pray in such a way that we treat others as we would have them treat us. We measure others by the same standard by which we wish to be measured (Matthew 7:2).

God may allow us to go through suffering and hardship so we can identify with those who suffer (2 Corinthians 1:3–5). It is easier to pray for someone if we have gone through a similar experience. We can relate to their situation.

There are also times when the Lord may let us feel another's suffering to better intercede for them. Many Christians have testified to actually experiencing the emotional stress, sorrow, pain, or joy of others as they were praying for them. This is probably a rare occurrence, but it does happen.

Some years ago as I was driving home on the freeway, looking up at the sky and thinking how beautiful it was, I suddenly knew without a doubt that at the exact moment a Christian brother was being taken to his death. He too was looking at the sky, but knowing that in a few seconds he would be with the Lord.

I started crying uncontrollably and had to pull my car over as I felt a great surge of pain and loss concerning this brother. I literally began to feel his fear, his desire to see his wife, and his concern for his children.

I did not know what else to do so I started praying for this brother and his family for some time, until this burden lifted.

I will admit I was quite stunned and bewildered by what had taken place, but I was also deeply moved that the Lord would use me in that desperate moment. As I was praying, I know God was using me, and His power was being released into this situation. Many may doubt my experience, but I know what happened. In the 30+ years I have been a Christian, this has happened only once, but I would welcome God using me in this manner again anytime.

9. When we pray, God releases His power and authority into people's lives and circumstances.

When King Hezekiah prayed for deliverance, great power was released from God that utterly destroyed the Assyrian army—185,000 of them. (2 Kings 19)

King Jehoshaphat prayed for deliverance from the Moabites and Ammonites. As a result, God's power was released, the enemy destroyed, and Israel was three days taking the spoils (2 Chronicles 20).

Nehemiah prayed that King Artaxerxes would allow him to go and rebuild Jerusalem. God influenced the King's heart, and Nehemiah was sent to rebuild the city (Nehemiah 1 & 2).

When Paul and Silas prayed, power was released that caused an earthquake, freeing them from prison (Acts 16:23–26).

When Peter prayed for Aeneas, power was released for his healing. Then, Peter prayed again and power was released to resurrect Dorcas from the dead (Acts 9:32–42).

The list could go on and on.

When we pray, God's power, authority, and influence are brought into our situations. The hope for the Church, our families, unsaved friends, and our country is intercessory prayer. We Christians must get down on our knees, repent of our sin and the sins of others, and ask God to bring His influence, conviction, and anointing upon our churches, communities, and nation.

The world will experience the Kingdom of God if and when God's people become the salt of the earth. When we exercise our God-given authority, particularly in prayer, and take back the territory lost to Satan, God will bring revival and heal our land.

PRAYER CHANGES THINGS!

We are Christ's ambassadors, and it is our job to bring the news of Christ's reconciliation to the world. However, we will never do this without being a people of prayer.

Why?

Because we can do nothing without God, and our way to God is through prayer.

God is the One Who prepares hearts, pulls down strongholds, convicts us of sin, and changes hearts. Our responsibility is to pray for His Kingdom to come and His will to be done, and then His power is released to accomplish His will on the earth.

Friend, start praying today that God's Kingdom will come to the world around you. As you pray, it will surely begin to happen. As you intercede, God will release His power into those circumstances or people for whom you are praying.

We have a God-given mandate to bring the Gospel to the world. Let us start doing it through intercessory prayer.

10. Intercession can be initiated by God.

The Lord will reveal things Himself or use others so we will intercede for people or situations.

In Genesis 18, God reveals to Abraham what He is about to do to Sodom and Gomorrah.

> *The Lord said, "Shall I hide from Abraham what I am about to do?" And the Lord said, "The outcry of Sodom and Gomorrah is indeed great, and their sin is exceedingly grave. I will go down now, and see if they have done entirely according to its outcry, which has come to Me."*
>
> (Genesis 18:17, 20–21)

When Abraham learned what God was about to do, his immediate response was to intercede for the cities (v.23).

In Exodus 32, God told Moses that He was going to destroy the Israelites because of their continued disobedience. As soon as Moses heard this, he entreated the Lord on the people's behalf, and God spared them.

Jesus told Peter that He had prayed so Peter's faith would not fail; it had been revealed to Jesus that Satan was about to attack Peter (Luke 22:31–32).

In Colossians 1:9, Paul, after hearing about the condition of the church at Colossi, writes,

> *For this reason also, since the day we heard of it, we have not ceased to pray for you and to ask that you may be filled with the knowledge of His will in all spiritual wisdom and understanding.*

We may not say it as eloquently as Paul, but there are times when the Lord burdens us to pray. How often have you heard others say "The Lord burdened me to pray," or "I felt led to pray for you"?

God revealed things to Abraham, Moses, Jesus, and Paul because He knew they would intercede for those situations.

God has not changed.

God still reveals things to His people so that they will intercede on behalf of others, releasing His influence into that situation. I doubt that anyone will ever understand why God has willed that intercession releases His power into the world. Why can't He just do what He wants done without first asking us to pray?

It is a mystery to me.

My main thought on this mystery is that perhaps God wants us to learn responsibility for others and to share in the battle as well as the victory. Whatever the reason, we know that prayer and intercession release God's power, influence, strength, wisdom, healing, and direction into people and circumstances.

As Christians, we are called to pray, and our prayers do make a difference. Prayer brings God's will into the world.

It is my hope that in this generation, we (God's people) will recommit ourselves to prayer, the only force that will bring renewal to the Church and revival to our country.

CHAPTER FOURTEEN

Developing a Prayer Life

PART 1

Preparation for Prayer

It is vital that we all develop a prayer discipline to increase our prayer lives and our effectiveness.

Because you are still reading this book, it is logical to assume that you are genuinely concerned about increasing your own prayer life. You understand that prayer brings you closer to Jesus and that it releases God's influence into your family, community, church, and city.

Over the past ten years I have read many books, attended numerous conferences, and given frequent messages on the subject of prayer. As a result of these endeavors, the Lord has taught me some keys to developing a consistent prayer life—and that is the subject of my final two chapters in the book. As you read these chapters, my prayer for you is that they will stimulate you to greater times of prayer and greater consistency in your prayer life.

Remember, time spent in prayer is never wasted.

Every minute spent with God has eternal value. Prayer is truly the single most important activity of our Christian life.

Pray—Especially If You Are Busy

The most common question I hear concerning developing a consistent prayer life is: "When am I supposed to pray? I'm so busy!"

Friend, the busier you are, the more important prayer becomes.

The busier my day, the more important it is that I begin it in prayer. I have learned the hard way that I must always make room for prayer. The times I have skipped it I have not accomplished as much, done as well, or been as effective as when I first set aside time to be alone with God.

It may not sound logical, but when we have a heavy schedule, spending time in prayer does not deplete the time we have to accomplish our work; it makes us more efficient and productive.

When we humble ourselves before God, asking for His wisdom, direction, and inspiration, we can accomplish far more then we can without His help.

The Apostle Paul, in the book of Ephesians, prays that the *"eyes of your hearts may be enlightened"* to *"what is the surpassing greatness of His power toward us who believe."*

When we pray, it releases God's supernatural power and influence into our day and circumstances.

THE TIME AND PLACE TO PRAY

It is essential to establish both a <u>place</u> and a <u>time</u> to pray. Jesus said,

> *But you, when you pray, go into your inner room, close your door and pray to your Father who is in secret, and your Father who sees what is done in secret will reward you.*

(Matthew 6:6)

Jesus told His disciples that if they wanted to pray, they should find a secret place where they could be alone with God. This place of prayer should be comfortable and convenient so that praying there will fit easily into your day. I know one man who gets up early and locks himself in the bathroom. You may select a closet, a spare bedroom, or a comfortable chair in the living room. I know one man who parks his car in a vacant lot and prays. Some take walks to be alone and pray.

Pick a place where you will not be interrupted as you pray, remembering that where you go is not as important as consistently going to that place.

That is why it is vital to pick a time when we can pray. For the majority of us, the best time seems to be the morning. If selecting the morning for your prayer means that you get up a little earlier, then my suggestion is "Do it. It is worth it!"

If you try consistently praying in the morning for six months, I guarantee your relationship with God and His influence in your life will increase! In Psalm 5:3, David writes:

> *In the morning, O Lord, You will hear my voice; in the morning I will order my prayer to You and eagerly watch.*

Starting off the day in prayer sets the tone for all that follows. We are able to lift up our daily activities, our relationships and tasks before the Lord, asking for His help.

The morning is the best time to rebuke the enemy from our day and ask God to give us wisdom, patience, and anointing for the day's tasks.

My former secretary possessed an uncanny ability of knowing the days I came into the church office without first spending time in prayer. After an incident in the office or on the phone, she would comment with a little twinkle in her eye, "Dave, you didn't take time to pray today, did you?"

She was not being judgmental. She honestly cared about me and the church, and knew it was important that I spend time alone with God before I tackled that day's work.

If early morning does not work for you, then pick a time that does. If getting alone with the Lord at noon or in the evening works out best for you, then please do it.

I've had several Christians tell me they are so groggy in the morning that trying to pray is almost futile. They prefer to pray in the evening when their mind is sharper.

The time of day we pray is not as important as developing a specific time and place to pray on a regular basis. If you do not set a time and a particular place to pray each day, it is very difficult to develop a prayer life.

SCHEDULED PRAYER

It has been helpful for me to commit myself to attending weekly church prayer meetings and to pray with a group of pastors once a month. By doing this, I have scheduled myself to pray regularly through the week no matter what else happens.

There will be times when you do not feel like praying, but if you schedule prayer times where you meet others, you will thwart the enemy's plans to keep you from prayer.

Set aside a certain amount of time to pray and be alone with God.

You may consider scheduling prayer as legalistic or forced, and you might be thinking to yourself, "Pastor Dave, I'd rather be led by the Spirit when to pray."

So would I!

But because of our weak human nature, I believe it is important to schedule a specific amount of time each day. This seems to be a necessary task for most of us who are striving to become men and women of faithful prayer.

Many mornings I simply do not feel like praying, but I have learned to do it anyway because I am committed to pray a set amount of time before starting each day.

The same is true in other disciplines.

If you want to learn how to play the piano, you must decide to practice every day—whether you feel like it or not. Learning to play the piano takes discipline and work. If you are not determined to set a daily routine, a million distractions will hinder your practice. After an initial burst of activity, your unscheduled practice times will dwindle.

Surely you do not believe that you can learn how to pray if you do not commit yourself to praying a specific amount of time each day. Prayer, like any other discipline, requires work and time for us to become proficient.

PRAY WITH CONFIDENCE

We should begin our prayers with a confidence that as we ask and wait on God in perseverance, He will act.

For from days of old they have not heard or perceived by ear, nor has the eye seen a God besides You, who acts in behalf of the one who waits for Him.

(Isaiah 64:4)

And without faith it is impossible to please Him, for he who comes to God must believe that He is and that He is a rewarder of those who seek Him.

(Hebrews 11:6)

This is the confidence which we have before Him, that, if we ask anything according to His will, He hears us. And if we know that He hears us in whatever we ask, we know that we have the requests which we have asked from Him.

(1 John 5:14–15)

As a Christian, you and I need to get one question settled in our minds: Is the Bible the Word of God or isn't it?

Can God's Word be trusted?

Can we base our lives on the promises that are in the Bible?

In short, do you really believe that the Bible is the inspired Word of God?

If you do, then you will approach prayer with great expectation and faith because the Bible says that God hears and answers our prayers. Even if you do not see things change immediately in the physical realm, you will still know that God is acting, moving, and influencing the person or situation you have lifted before Him.

HINDRANCES TO PRAYER

As we become serious about our prayer lives, we must understand that there are things that hinder our prayers.

Remember, prayer in its purest form is simply talking to God. It is sharing concerns, joys, fears, etc. with a loving Father.

The Bible clearly tells us that if there are certain attitudes or characteristics evident in our lives, it hinders God from responding to our prayers.

Consider a father who deeply loves his daughter, but she has stolen a large amount of money from him. Won't her action cause a serious rift between the two? If a son continually disobeys his father, won't his disobedience affect their relationship?

I realize these are not perfect examples, but hopefully you understand the truth expressed.

In the following pages, I want to share with you six major hindrances that affect our prayers before God.

HINDRANCE ONE: SIN

Your iniquities have made a separation between you and your God, and your sins have hidden His face from you so that He does not hear.

(Isaiah 59:2)

For the eyes of the Lord are toward the righteous, and His ears attend to their prayer, but the face of the Lord is against those who do evil.

(1 Peter 3:12)

Other references: Psalm 34:15–16; Isaiah 1:12–15; Psalm 66:18.

HINDRANCE TWO: IDOLS OF THE HEART

For your gods are as many as your cities, O Judah; and as many as the streets of Jerusalem are the altars you have set... Therefore do not pray for this people, nor lift up a cry or prayer for them; for I will not listen when they call to Me because of their disaster.

(Jeremiah 11:13–14)

An idol is any object, person, or personal ambition that consumes the thoughts of one's life.

As Christians, our Lord Jesus must have the preeminent place in our lives.

If anything causes you to disobey or not believe the Word of God, chances are you have an idol in your life. If something dominates your thinking and how you respond to life, then you need to repent of that thing and truly make Jesus the Lord of your life.

Some examples of possible idols are: the love of money, the desire for prestige, extreme infatuation with someone of the opposite sex, a time-stealing form of recreation, the obsessive seeking of possessions, an extreme commitment to a philosophy or an organization, or an unhealthy relationship which you do not want to end.

HINDRANCE THREE: LACK OF GIVING TO GOD AND THOSE IN NEED

We are specifically commanded by God's Word to give tithes and offerings to God. In the book of Malachi, God gives the Israelites a list of reasons why their relationship with Him had been affected. One of the reasons was that they had robbed God (Malachi 3:7–12).

In the U.S. and the western world, finances are the major area where many Christians stubbornly refuse to obey God. I realize this hindrance could have been included in the hindrance of sin, but many Christians strive to walk holy before God in all but this one area.

As a pastor, I have heard just about every excuse you can imagine for not tithing, but excuses do not work with God. If you are not tithing, you are in sin and this will affect your prayers before God.

Proverb 21:13 shows that God also expects us to help those in need, and reveals His heart toward those who have the means but refuse to help the needy.

> *He who shuts his ear to the cry of the poor will also cry himself and not be answered.*

My friend, if you want to experience an intimate relationship with God and see your prayers answered, be obedient in trusting God fully with your finances.

HINDRANCE FOUR: UNFORGIVENESS

Unforgiveness in our hearts towards another will affect our prayers before God. In Matthew 5:23–24, Jesus tells His disciples that before they go and offer their offerings at the altar, they should be reconciled to that person who has something against them. In the Gospel of Mark, Jesus' words are recorded for us concerning this matter.

Whenever you stand praying, forgive, if you have anything against anyone, so that your Father who is in heaven will also forgive you your transgressions.

(Mark 11:25)

When we have unforgiveness against another, our relationship with our Lord will be affected. This iniquity (sin) will cause a separation and distance between us and God.

Unforgiveness is a key hindrance to prayer because Christians often refuse to let go of anger and bitterness toward a person who has truly wronged them. This unforgiveness is an affront to God for two reasons:

1. Jesus died for that other person and loves them (Romans 2:11), and

2. God expects you to love and pray for them and their situation (John 3:16; 1 John 3:17-19).

If you are serious about becoming a man or woman of prayer, recognize any unforgiveness in your heart toward another, repent of this sin, then forgive and make amends where possible.

HINDRANCE FIVE: WRONG RELATIONS BETWEEN HUSBAND AND WIFE

The Bible has given both the husband and wife specific commands concerning their attitudes and responsibilities toward their mate. These commands are clearly spelled out in Ephesians 5:22–23. The wife is called to submit to the spiritual authority God placed on her husband, and the husband is to be the spiritual head of the home, leading it by serving. When either of these two basic requirements is missing from a Christian marriage, it conflicts with God's plan and results in a miserable marriage.

In 1 Peter 3:1–2 Peter tells the wife:

> *You wives, be submissive to your own husbands so that even if any of them are disobedient to the word, they may be won without a word by the behavior of the wives, as they observe your chaste and respectful behavior.*

The wife's main responsibility in a marriage is to be submissive to her husband. This submission is not simply to a man (her husband), but to the spiritual authority God has given her husband. It is an attitude of the heart, not a decision that does away with a woman's opinion or personality. If you are a wife and are serious about prayer, check your attitude concerning your husband. If your feelings for your husband are not what they should be, confess this to God, repent and seek counsel if necessary.

In verse 7 of 1 Peter 3, Peter gives a warning that should be very sobering for any Christian husband:

> *You husbands in the same way, live with your wives in an understanding way, as with someone weaker, since she is a woman; and show her honor as a fellow heir of the grace of life, so that your prayers will not be hindered.*

If a husband has not taken on his spiritual leadership, abdicated his responsibilities in the home, or verbally or physically abuses his wife, his prayers will be hindered.

After many years in the pastorate, I am convinced that the greatest problem in most Christian marriages is the husband refusing to set the spiritual example. When the husband is doing his best to be the spiritual leader, love his wife, and lead his family, generally there is a good marriage.

If you are a husband and are serious about prayer, how you treat your wife is of utmost importance if you desire to pray with effectiveness.

Hindrance Six: Unbelief

One of the biggest changes in how I pray for direction, wisdom and anointing came after doing a study on James 1:5–8.

> *But if any of you lacks wisdom, let him ask of God, who gives to all generously and without reproach, and it will be given to him. But he must ask in faith without any doubting, for the one who doubts is like the surf of the sea, driven and tossed by the wind. For that man ought not to expect that he will receive anything from the Lord, being a double-minded man, unstable in all his ways.*

When we pray we must have faith that God hears us and will answer our prayers. Otherwise, we will be constantly doubting His intervention in our lives, and will be unwilling to step out in faith to do His work.

After I pray for God's guidance, wisdom, etc., I now understand that I must boldly take steps of faith that correspond to my prayers. If I fail to do so, what I receive from God will be greatly diminished. Jesus addresses this issue in Mark 11:24.

> *Therefore I say to you, all things for which you pray and ask, believe that you have received them, and they will be granted you.*

This principal of prayer is qualified by Jesus in His other teachings (Matthew 6:10; Mark 14:36) and by the Apostle John (1 John 5:14–15).

The message is clear: faith pleases God (Hebrews 11:6), and unbelief hinders prayers.

Do not be deceived.

If you ignore God's wishes in any of these six areas, it will definitely hinder your prayers. Far too many Christians refuse to deal with these issues and then wonder, "Why does God seem so distant?"

If you are serious about being a man or woman of prayer, sin must be confessed and dealt with. There is no compromising on God's behalf.

In conclusion, let me urge you to decide on a place and a specific time to pray. Then, deal with any area that would hinder your prayers. As you pray, believe that God answers prayers and is the rewarder of those who seek Him.

CHAPTER FIFTEEN

Developing a Prayer Life

PART 2

Practical Suggestions on How to Pray

In Psalm 5:3, David says "*In the morning I will order my prayer to You.*"

Before I walk out the front door, I have found it very important to set my day in order through prayer. Even if praying in the morning is difficult and you have set aside another part of your day to pray, I would still suggest you spend a few minutes in prayer each morning.

In our family, we all gather around and take a few minutes and pray for each other's day. Both my wife and I definitely notice a difference in how our days go when we consistently begin each day in prayer.

Who would argue that we live in an evil and perverse generation?

Peter tells us that Satan is like a prowling lion seeking someone to devour (1 Peter 5:8). Ephesians 6:12 tells us that our struggles are,

> *...not against flesh and blood, but against the rulers, against the powers, against the world forces of this darkness, against the spiritual forces of wickedness.*

Since prayer gives us power over the enemy, doesn't it seem logical that before leaving our homes each morning we should commit our day to God, binding the enemy, and asking for God's protection?

I pray with my children twice each day—once in the morning before we all go our separate ways, and once in the evening before we go to bed. I do not do this as just a ritual or because I believe it to be a neat thing to do with my kids. I do it because I know that our prayers for one another truly do bind the enemy in our lives. (Matthew 16:19)

Do not ever underestimate the power that prayer (if only for a few minutes each morning) will have on your day. Frankly, I do not want to give the enemy any opportunity to try to pollute my life or the lives of my family.

You may ask, "How can just a short prayer in the morning make such a difference?"

As we commit our day to God, it is an act of humility that declares our dependence upon Him. The Bible clearly tells us that God will strengthen and protect those who humbly live before Him (James 4:6,10; 1 Peter 5:6).

At this point in the book, hopefully you have found a place to pray and set aside a specific amount of time to pray.

What next?

Well, if you are like most of us, you get up in the morning (or whatever time you have set) and go to your place of prayer and begin to pray. After ten or twelve minutes of praying for your family, church, friends, city, and nation, you run out of things to say.

Do not become discouraged.

You are not alone.

I remember struggling with the same thing when I first became serious about spending time alone with God in prayer.

To combat this problem, I have listed ten practical suggestions on how to develop a prayer life. If you implement them, I believe they will significantly increase your prayers and deeply enrich your time before God.

PRACTICAL HELP #1

Use the Lord's Prayer as an outline.

Quite a few years ago I read a pamphlet by Larry Lea challenging Christians to use the Lord's Prayer as a basic prayer outline. This suggestion impressed me, so I began using the Lord's prayer as my guide. This was the initial breakthrough that really began to help me increase my prayer time.

In Luke 11, Jesus' disciples asked Him to teach them how to pray. They had seen Jesus being alone with God in prayer, and realized that these prayers guided Him, providing direction for where Jesus went and what He said. Prayer produced the power evidenced in His life. Prayer energized Jesus' ministry.

The disciples witnessed that before Jesus made a decision, He would always spend time alone with God (Luke 6:12–16). In response to His disciples' request, Jesus taught them what we now call "The Lord's Prayer."

In Matthew 6:9, Jesus tells His disciples to *"Pray, then, in this way,"* then gives them His prayer. He did not say, "Pray this prayer over and over again one hundred times," or "Pray this prayer through one time and you are done." He said, "Pray in this way." In other words, use this prayer as a basic outline.

To follow the suggestion that Jesus gave His disciples, I would advise that you recite one sentence of the Lord's Prayer at a time, then simply talk to God about all the things that fall under that particular category.

To illustrate, let me briefly examine the six phrases in Jesus' prayer and explain how I use them to pray.

Phrase One: *"Our Father who is in Heaven, hallowed be Your name" (v.9).*

Jesus is suggesting that our prayers should begin with honor and worship to God.

Start out your prayer by thanking God for all He has done in your life. You might want to sing Him a worship song or read a praise Psalm. You might want to simply raise your hands and worship Him in silence. If the Lord has given you the gift of tongues, why not use it to praise Him?

One of the best ways to worship God is to simply renew your commitment to following Him as your Lord.

I have found that if I start my prayer in the worship of God, it puts my life and the world around me in proper perspective.

Phrase Two: *"Your kingdom come" (v.10).*

Pray that God's influence, His reality would spread to all your family, to those at work, at church, in the city, the media, schools, etc. I routinely ask God to heal the sick, reap a harvest of souls, influence those in public office, that His Spirit would fall on the Church, that He would rebuke demonic strongholds over our city, that a conviction for sin would fall on the Church and the city, that He would raise up godly people in the media, etc.

In short, I pray for revival.

Phrase Three: *"Your will be done" (v.11).*

Confess the fact that Jesus is your Lord and recommit your life to Him. Express your sincere desire to manifest His will in your life. Commit yourself to obedience and submission to His word. Ask God's help to understand His will, His way in every circumstance of the day. Pray that His will would come about in the particular lives and situations that are on your heart.

Remember, when we pray according to His will, *"we have the requests which we have asked from Him"* (1 John 5:15).

I do not know if I will ever understand it, but God has ordained that somehow our prayers play a part in the bringing of His will into existence (1 Timothy 2:1–4). As you develop a prayer life and your knowledge of God increases, He will begin to share His heart with you. You will literally be burdened to pray for the things that burden God.

Phrase Four: *"Give us this day our daily bread" (v.11).*

This is where we pray for our own needs, petitioning God for our-selves or our families. There may be a family member who needs salvation, wisdom in making a decision, employment, business opportunities, financial concerns—the list is endless. By limiting our personal concerns to this part of our prayer time, it helps us not to focus solely on prayers centered on ourselves.

Phrase Five: *"And forgive us our debts, as we also have forgiven our debtors" (v.12).*

Ask the Lord to forgive your sins, and explore the ways in which you may have fallen short of His plans for your life. It is good to examine your heart to see if there is unforgiveness or bitterness towards anyone. This is an appropriate time to place personal offenses at the Lord's feet and commit yourself to walking in forgiveness.

Scripture clearly tells us to walk in forgiveness so that *"no advantage would be taken of us by Satan"* (2 Corinthians 2:10–11).

God's Word commands us to "love your enemies and pray for those who persecute you" (Matthew 5:44).

Phrase Six: *"And do not lead us into temptation, but deliver us from evil" (v.13).*

Ask God not to let you be brought into a place of temptation you cannot handle. Ask the Lord to protect you from the strategies and schemes of the devil.

Daily I ask God to let me clearly see the enemy's plan to try to pull me into sin, bringing shame to the Kingdom of God. I usually pray something like this: "Lord, you know my weaknesses. Let my weaknesses become my strengths in resisting temptations." I frequently ask God to help me turn and run from all forms of temptation, just as Joseph ran from Potiphar's wife (Genesis 39).

Pray for strength, wisdom and discernment to turn away from evil. Ask God to help you see *"the way of escape"* that He will provide in times of temptation (1 Corinthians 10:13), and affirm your belief that *"the Lord knows how to rescue the godly from temptation"* (2 Peter 2:9).

Jesus gave His disciples the Lord's Prayer as an outline so that we would understand how to pray. Therefore, we should follow His model prayer to help us go before God's throne with greater focus.

Practical Help #2

Pray through devotional Psalms (Psalm 25, 26, 27, 40, 41, 42, 43, 45, 63, 65, 69, 84) and other scriptures.

One scripture that has become my own prayer to God is Psalm 25. I read one verse at a time and make it my personal prayer to the Father. In Psalm 25, David starts by declaring his trust in God (v.1–3).

I do the same.

David asks God to "*make me know Your ways… teach me Your paths*" (v.4). I ask God to help me know His will and His way in all areas of my day.

David proclaims that God "*leads the humble in justice, and He teaches the humble His way*" (v.9). I pray for a humble heart, not wanting to think more highly of myself than I should (Romans 12:3).

In verses 12–13, David speaks of the fear of the Lord because it will bring instruction and reveal God's hidden wisdom. I usually spend some time praying for God's fear to be upon my life because I know the fear of the Lord is the beginning of wisdom (Proverbs 1:7).

Many Psalms are beautiful prayers, fitting almost every circumstance. I find it very helpful to use one of David's Psalms (prayers), and make it my own when I am weary, perplexed, or unable to find the appropriate words.

May I suggest you begin reading through the Psalms, and as you read, mark the ones that are obviously prayers, and note the situation they address. Then you can use them to pray for those specific situations at the appropriate times in your life.

Many scriptures can be used to pray for ourselves and others. For example, in Isaiah 50:4–5, the prophet says,

> *The Lord God has given me the tongue of disciples, that I may know how to sustain the weary one with a word. He awakens me morning by morning. He awakens my*

ear to listen as a disciple. The Lord God has opened my
ear; and I was not disobedient, nor did I turn back.

I have prayed many times that the Lord would give me the tongue of
a disciple so I could sustain the weary with a word, giving wise counsel.
I pray that pertinent verses come to my mind when I counsel people,
also asking the Lord to open my ears to listen as a disciple, and to have
the courage to obey when I know His will.

In 1 Kings 3:9, King Solomon asks God to...

... give Your servant an understanding heart... to discern
between good and evil.

Again, you can simply make this prayer your own. Remember, in
verse 10 it says that this prayer was *"pleasing in the sight of the Lord."*

The verses in the Bible that can be made into prayers for you
or others are almost endless, but here are just a few to help you get
started: Ephesians 1:17–18; 3:14–21; Acts 4:29–30; 2 Thessalonians
3:5; Colossians 1:9–11.

PRACTICAL HELP #3

Pray through a prayer list.

Using a prayer list has been very helpful in keeping my prayers
focused and in keeping my mind from wandering.

Making a list of people and situations for intercession can be
very rewarding as you see God answer your prayers. A list keeps you
accountable to pray for those people and situations you promised to
pray for, and it is a great encouragement and witness as they see God's
intervention in their lives, realizing that you have been praying for
them.

Let me recommend a few things about your prayer list.

1. Write down the results of your prayers. It will be a great blessing to you.

2. Try to keep the list a manageable size, taking into consideration the available time you have set aside to pray.

3. Make a new prayer list every week or two so your prayers do not begin to feel repetitious. There may be a few things you leave on the list, but I would still suggest you change the list regularly to assure your interest level remains high.

PRACTICAL HELP #4

Pray out loud and close your eyes.

When I pray silently, it is much harder to keep my mind from wandering and becoming sleepy. Praying out loud definitely helps me keep alert and organize my thoughts. Of course, there are times to be silent before the Lord, but if we pray silently too often, our minds tend to wander, and if we are tired, it is easy to fall asleep.

If you still find that you are getting drowsy when you pray, try walking around while you pray out loud. My brother prays this way all the time. It is not necessary to pray out loud, but I believe it helps to make us more effective.

Praying out loud is also important when we rebuke demonic strongholds or influences. As I discussed in Chapter 5, we must rebuke and pray against the demonic because life's battles are first won in the spiritual world before they manifest in our physical world.

The Bible tells us, *"For You alone know the hearts of the sons of men"* (2 Chronicles 6:30). This tells me that the devil and his demons do not know exactly what we are thinking and cannot hear us when we pray silently.

Therefore, it seems logical to pray out loud when we rebuke and bind all aspects of the kingdom of darkness.

I suggest that you close your eyes; it does help concentration since it eliminates distractions you otherwise might see. I am NOT saying that you cannot pray with your eyes open. I pray with my eyes open occasionally as I pace back and forth in a room. It has simply been my experience that closing my eyes helps me zero in on the task of prayer.

Practical Help #5

Remind God of His promises.

In Isaiah 62:6–7 we read,

> *On your walls, O Jerusalem, I have appointed watchmen;*
> *all day and night they will never keep silent. You who*
> *remind the Lord, take no rest for yourselves; and give*
> *Him no rest until He establishes and makes Jerusalem*
> *a praise in the earth.*

Isaiah was telling the watchmen to remind God of His specific promises to establish Israel. Reminding God of His promises is an effective way of praying for God's will to be accomplished.

You may ask, "Does God really need to be reminded of His promises?"

Of course not, but these types of prayers please God because they proclaim our trust in Him.

For example, if you need direction in understanding whether or not to accept a business opportunity, I would suggest you remind God that in Psalm 32:8 He promised,

> *[to] teach you in the way which you should go; I will counsel you with My eye upon you.*

You could pray:

"Lord, I don't know what to do in this situation, but You have promised to teach me in the way I should go, and counsel me. So, I believe You will instruct me concerning this decision."

Or, you may find yourself facing financial hardship.

This would be an appropriate time to prayerfully remind God of His promises in Malachi 3:7–12.192.

"Lord, You promised that if I was faithful with my tithes and offerings, You would bless me. Lord, in faith I ask You to bless my finances."

In times of temptation, you may want to pray,

"Lord, Your Word says that during times of temptation you will *'provide the way of escape... that* [I] *will be able to endure it.'* Lord, *show me the way of escape in this situation.*"

There are hundreds of promises in the Word of God fitting almost every conceivable situation.

I suggest you go to the Bible bookstore in your area and buy a book that lists God's promises for your life; there are numerous ones published. The one I have in my office has been a great blessing to me over the years.

Of course, memorizing verses is the most beneficial since God can then bring them to your mind during times of prayer.

PRACTICAL HELP #6

If you have the gift of tongues, use it.

I have already shared with you how invaluable the gift of tongues has been to me in my prayer times, especially when I want to continue to pray about a particular situation or person but have run out of things to pray. During these times, I simply pray in tongues and let the Holy Spirit pray through me (Romans 8:26).

If you are serious about prayer, perhaps you should consider asking God to give you the gift of tongues. Remember, the Apostle Paul said, *"desire earnestly spiritual gifts"* (1 Corinthians 14:1). Paul tells the Corinthians that he speaks in tongues more than any of them (1 Corinthians 14:18).

Isn't it plausible to assume that Paul used tongues during his prayer times?

Please, do not be afraid of this gift. You might consider praying this simple prayer:

"Lord, please give me this gift of speaking in tongues if it will help me in my prayer life."

PRACTICAL HELP #7

Take time for silence and listen for God.

I have written at great length concerning hearing the voice of God in prayer in Chapter 7. In this section, I want to concentrate on hearing God's voice by being silent before the Lord during prayer. Our silence before God outwardly demonstrates reverence, humility, and a total dependence on Him (Psalm 62). It shows a willingness not to be hasty with our own wishes but manifests a desire to wait on God for His purposes.

There are several places in Scripture where men have fallen on their faces before God in silence (Revelation 1:17; Daniel 8:17–18; 10:9). In the book of Revelation there is complete silence in heaven for half an hour as heaven waits for God.

Learning to be silent before God is a good discipline that helps put our lives in perspective when compared to our Lord and His Kingdom.

PRACTICAL HELP #8

Imagine yourself at a place of prayer before God.

If you find you are having trouble concentrating and it seems your prayers are bouncing off the ceiling, try visualizing yourself talking to God.

Many times I find it difficult to pray the way I desire. At these times, I visualize myself on my knees before the throne of God, beginning to talk to our Lord, releasing the burdens on my heart. I do not actually see the Lord on a throne (I have read descriptions of the throne of God in Revelation, and it is beyond my ability to comprehend). Instead, I see only a bright light and myself kneeling before the light coming from the throne. This method has helped me many times to concentrate and experience a productive and intimate time of prayer with God.

I remember reading somewhere that someone imagined themselves in a green meadow talking with the Lord, surrounded by His presence. Others visualize themselves alone on a mountain with the Lord.

The place you choose does not matter.

Just develop a place in your mind that you can go to and be alone with God. This is beneficial when you are having trouble concentrating, and at times when you are surrounded by noise and people.

I realize this may sound a bit mystical and weird to some of you. But, I am convinced it is important to develop your own, private place of prayer in your mind to be alone with God. This place enables you to experience an intimate relationship and conversation with God at a moment's notice.

Of course, I am not suggesting that it is absolutely necessary to have an intimate place to fellowship with God, only that it has been helpful to me and many others.

PRACTICAL HELP #9

Be honest and truthful about your feelings.

I acknowledged my sin to You, and my iniquity I did not hide.

(Psalm 32:5)

If you are serious about prayer, then you must approach God in truth. God knows how you feel, your thoughts, and if you harbor bitterness, anger, or jealousy.

Why pretend with God?

I have always thought this was foolish because God is omniscient (all knowing). God knows all His creation (Psalm 147:4). He's aware if even one sparrow falls to the ground (Matthew 10:29) and knows the number of hairs on your head (Matthew 10:30). He knows the will and work of every man (Psalm 33:13–15) and the thoughts of men (Psalm 139:2). He knows men's hearts (1 Kings 8:39).

When I pray, I let God know how I really feel about people and situations. I even share when I am upset with Him. I might as well confess these things because God already knows my every thought.

There have been a few times when I have been very angry at God, perplexed at how He was handling a particular situation.

Are these feelings good?

Of course not!

But in my honesty with God it becomes that much easier for the Lord to bring conviction and repentance to my heart. When I am open, the sin that was affecting my relationship with the Lord is confessed and forgiven.

Practical Help #10

Allow for spontaneous praying.

It is a good practice during your prayer time to ask God, "Is there anything that You would like me to pray about?"

If you are like me, you want to be used by the Lord and pray the prayers that are on His heart. So why not ask the Lord to bring to your mind people and situations that need prayer? After you ask, listen. If something or someone comes to your mind, pray for that person or situation.

There have been times when, after asking God that question, I have had individuals from our church, situations in the city, other churches in the area, or family members come to my mind. If I ask the Lord to bring people and situations to my mind, and things do come, I pray for them.

SPONTANEOUS PRAYER

Please be warned, it is my experience that if you try to develop a prayer life solely with spontaneous prayer, you will not accomplish much.

Why?

Because *"the Spirit is willing but the flesh is weak."* There will be times when you do not feel like praying, and very little will come to your mind.

The inevitable outcome is a very short and ineffective prayer.

Spontaneous prayer in a group setting works rather well as each person prays and the others agree. But, in one's private prayer time, spontaneous prayer will not accomplish as much as a disciplined prayer life.

As I conclude this book, I pray you have received some practical wisdom on how you can develop your prayer life with God. Hopefully, you have read some things that will help you discipline yourself to regularly get alone and pray.

It is my prayer that you would know God intimately and be used to bring about His Kingdom in your family, church, city, and the world.

My sincere hope for you is that your prayer time would become an exciting time of refreshing, anointing, and ministry to you, your family, the world around you, and would hasten an outpouring of God's Spirit in our land. Remember, prayer is the single most important activity of your Christian life.

STUDY
GUIDE

Week One

Read Chapters 1–2.

Chapter 1 – "Prayer: The Beginning"

1. Why is prayer such an important activity in our Christian life?

_____

_____

_____

_____

_____

2. What is the basic reason the Church is not winning America for Christ?

_____

_____

_____

_____

_____

3. What Scripture holds the key to the lack of spiritual power being released in individuals and the Church?

_____

_____

_____

_____

_____

4. Has prayer been a struggle for you? If so, why?

_____

_____

_____

_____

_____

5. Why does consistent prayer produce godly characteristics?

_____

_____

_____

_____

CHAPTER 2 – "DO YOU BELIEVE IN PRAYER?"

1. According to Pastor David Hoffman, what does he believe
    the Lord told him was the reason so many Christians don't
    pray?

    _____

    _____

    _____

    _____

    _____

2. When we Christians find ourselves in overwhelming
    circumstances we have three choices. What are they?

    _____

    _____

    _____

    _____

    _____

3. In 2 Chronicles 20:15 King Jehoshaphat is told by a prophet
    "The battle is not yours but God's." Why is this an important
    principle?

    _____

    _____

    _____

    _____

    _____

4. What will the Lord do if we wait on Him in any situation?

_____

_____

_____

_____

_____

5. After reading this chapter, how would you answer the question "Do you believe in prayer?"

_____

_____

_____

_____

_____

Week Two

Read Chapters 3–4.

Chapter 3 – "Prayer Changes Things"

1. Why is it important that we know how God dealt with the
    early Church?

    _____

    _____

    _____

    _____

    _____

2. Why must our first reaction to circumstances in our lives
    always be prayer?

    _____

    _____

    _____

    _____

    _____

3. In your own words, what do you think E. M. Bounds meant when He said, "Prayer puts God to work?"

_____

_____

_____

_____

_____

4. How can we be sure that God will act on our prayers?

_____

_____

_____

_____

_____

5. Give an example in your own life how prayer has changed a situation.

_____

_____

_____

_____

_____

CHAPTER 4 – "PERSEVERING IN PRAYER"

1. According to 1 John 5:14–15, what prayer is always answered if we keep persisting in prayer?

   _____

   _____

   _____

   _____

   _____

2. How do we know that we are praying according to the will of God?

   _____

   _____

   _____

   _____

   _____

3. Why do so many Christians miss out on the blessings of God?

   _____

   _____

   _____

   _____

   _____

4. Give some examples of why Christians might give up praying.

_____

_____

_____

_____

_____

5. According to Luke 18:1, if we fail to pray in the midst of trials or difficult situations, what will happen?

_____

_____

_____

_____

_____

6. Give examples of how God has increased your faith, kept you from depression, and filled you with hope as you continued in prayer in the midst of a time of trial.

_____

_____

_____

_____

_____

Week Three

Read Chapters 5–6.

Chapter 5 – "Prayer As Spiritual Warfare"

1. Why does Satan put such a high priority on undermining our prayers?

_____

_____

_____

_____

_____

2. Why is the story of the Israelites' victory over the Amalekites in Exodus 17 critical in understanding the importance of prayer?

_____

_____

_____

_____

_____

3. Why are Jesus' words in Mark 3:27 important when praying for our nation? Why do we have power over the demonic? How should we pray against demonic influences and strongholds?

_____

_____

_____

_____

_____

_____

_____

_____

_____

4. Write down any strongholds or deceptions that you have identified in those you may be praying for, or even in a community (share with group).

_____

_____

_____

_____

_____

CHAPTER 6 – "PRAYER AND OBEDIENCE"

1. What is a major determining factor in how we will experience life?

_____

_____

_____

_____

_____

2. Why is obedience nothing more than faith in action?

_____

_____

_____

_____

_____

3. How is our obedience related to our intimacy with God?

_____

_____

_____

_____

_____

4. How would you define a lukewarm Christian?

_____

_____

_____

_____

_____

5. Why does sin and disobedience affect our prayers? Since sin does affect our prayers, what should our response be (James 5:16)?

_____

_____

_____

_____

_____

Week Four

Read Chapters 7–8.

Chapter 7 – "Hearing the Voice of God In Prayer"

1. How can we be sure that God speaks to His people? Which Scripture reference given in this chapter encouraged you?

_____

_____

_____

_____

_____

2. What is the single biggest obstacle in our pursuit of knowing God?

_____

_____

_____

_____

_____

3. What is a good fivefold method to begin practicing to hear the voice of God? Discuss this method with others in your group.

_____

_____

_____

_____

_____

4. Why is it important to use all of the eightfold tests to discern if you heard from God?

_____

_____

_____

_____

_____

5. Can you give examples of times you thought you had heard from God and didn't? Why do you think you made a mistake?

_____

_____

_____

_____

_____

CHAPTER 8 — "PRAYER FOR THE SICK AND HURTING"

1. Why do you think many Christians are reluctant to pray for physical healing?

_____

_____

_____

_____

_____

2. Jesus' ministry centered on two things; what were they?

_____

_____

_____

_____

_____

3. Finish this sentence: A disciple is someone who becomes like their _____.

4. Why do you believe the Church doesn't experience more miracles and healings?

_____

_____

_____

_____

_____

5. What type of faith will experience miracles through God's Holy Spirit?

_____

_____

_____

_____

_____

_____

_____

_____

_____

_____

_____

_____

_____

_____

_____

_____

_____

_____

_____

Week Five

Read Chapters 9–10.

Chapter 9 – "Answered vs. Unanswered Prayer"

Part One

1. Explain this sentence in your own words: What many Christians call "unanswered prayer" is really answered prayer; they just don't like the answer.

_____

_____

_____

_____

_____

2. Why is the knowledge that God answers our prayers so important to us as Christians?

_____

_____

_____

_____

3. What does it mean to pray in the Name of Jesus?

_____

_____

_____

_____

_____

4. Complete this sentence: The assurance (faith) that God is going to answer our prayers is grounded in

_____.

CHAPTER 10 – "ANSWERED VS. UNANSWERED PRAYER"

PART TWO

1. Have you ever thought God wasn't hearing you and your prayers were not being answered? If so, give examples.

_____

_____

_____

_____

_____

2. Do you believe any of your prayers have been hindered by any of the "Five Hindrances to Prayer?" If so, give an example.

_____

_____

_____

_____

_____

3. Complete this sentence:

Prayers are not always answered as we would like but they are always answered _____, never _____.

4. What does question #3 mean to you?

_____

_____

_____

_____

_____

5. What are the four ways Pastor David Hoffman believes God answers prayer? Do you agree with him? Why or why not?

1) _____

2) _____

3) _____

4) _____

_____

_____

_____

_____

_____

Week Six

Read Chapters 11–13.

Chapter 11 – "Prayer and Fasting"

1. As Christians, there is no command for us to fast in the Bible. While this is true, why should we still take fasting seriously?

_____

_____

_____

_____

_____

2. How do Christians use fasting to try to get what they want?

_____

_____

_____

_____

_____

3. How does fasting remind us of our dependence upon God?

_____

_____

_____

_____

_____

4. As fasting reminds us of our weakness, inability, and insufficiency without God, how does God respond to this acknowledgment?

_____

_____

_____

_____

_____

CHAPTER 12 – "PRAYER SOCIETY"

1. Jesus' disciples did not ask Jesus to teach them how to preach, evangelize, or do miracles. What did they ask Him to teach them? Why is this significant?

_____

_____

_____

_____

_____

2. What would keep Christians from making a commitment to the five pledges of the Prayer Society?

_____

_____

_____

_____

_____

3. Do you think challenging people to prayer 2 ½ hours a week is fair and realistic? Why or why not?

_____

_____

_____

_____

_____

CHAPTER 13 — "INTERCESSORY PRAYER"

1. How would you define intercessory prayer?

_____

_____

_____

_____

_____

2. Why does intercessory prayer proclaim one's dependence on God?

_____

_____

_____

_____

_____

3. In your opinion, why is intercessory prayer so important for the Christian community?

_____

_____

_____

_____

_____

4. What part of intercessory prayer was new to you? How will this influence your prayer life?

    _____

    _____

    _____

    _____

    _____

5. Give an example of how intercessory prayer has changed a situation, relationship, or a person's life.

    _____

    _____

    _____

    _____

    _____

Week Seven

Read Chapters 14–15.

"Developing a Prayer Life"

Part One: Preparation for Prayer

1. Why is it essential to find a time and a place to regularly pray?

_____

_____

_____

_____

_____

2. As Christians, why should we pray with confidence that our Lord will hear us?

_____

_____

_____

_____

_____

3. What hindrance to prayer do you think affects the most Christians? Why?

_____

_____

_____

_____

_____

4. Ask the Lord to reveal any hindrances to your prayers and to keep you from anything that would hinder your prayers before God.

_____

_____

_____

_____

_____

CHAPTER 15 – "DEVELOPING A PRAYER LIFE"

PART TWO: PRACTICAL SUGGESTIONS ON HOW TO PRAY

1. Why is it best for most people to pray first thing in the morning?

_____

_____

_____

_____

_____

2. Which one of the practical helps to prayer have you not used before?

_____

_____

_____

_____

_____

3. How has any one of the practical helps to prayer helped you develop a prayer life?

_____

_____

_____

_____

_____

4. In your own life, what is the hardest part to keeping a regular prayer time with God?

_____

_____

_____

_____

_____

5. Now that you've finished this book, what has God taught you about prayer?

_____

_____

_____

_____

_____

_____

_____

_____

_____

_____

_____

_____

_____

_____

_____

NOTES

Order Page

To order more copies of *Prayer Will Change Your World,* visit our website: www.foothillschurch.org or call (619) 442-7728.

Made in the USA
Columbia, SC
11 February 2022